UTTER
NONSENSE

Selected poems of
Lewis Carrol & Edward Lear

Lonely Scribe

Published by Lonely Scribe
www.lonelyscribe.co.uk

First published 2004

Cover design, typesetting and biographical notes
copyright © 2004 Armadillo Design Ltd

ISBN: 1-905179-00-6

Contents

EDWARD LEAR
(1812–1888)

Born in London in 1812, Edward Lear became famous as an artist and writer, though he did not always find it easy to support himself by his ventures. His first noted success came when he was commissioned to illustrate *The Family of the Psittacidae* (1832): his paintings of parrots were some of the first colour plates of animals produced in Britain and drew comparisons with the great Audubon.

It was on the back of this work that Lear was invited to Knowsley Hall in Cheshire to record for posterity the animals in the Earl of Derby's menagerie. Here, he discovered a gift for entertainment, and spent hours amusing the children of the house with his comic drawings and rhymes. In 1846 these verses, in what would become known as 'Limerick' form, found a wider audience as *A Book of Nonsense*.

Lear continued to write, to draw and to travel, though in later life deteriorating eyesight prevented him from pursuing the natural history illustration he so loved. He published several travel books, including *Sketches of Rome* (1842) and *Illustrated Excursions in Italy* (1846), embellished with his own paintings and drawings, but he also continued to tap the rich vein of fantastical imagination with which he was blessed.

As well as further short verses and drawings, Lear produced several longer works that have delighted children (and their parents) for generations to follow. *The Owl and the Pussy-cat*, *The Jumblies*, *The Dong with the Luminous Nose* and *The Quangle Wangle's Hat* are classics of children's literature, and Lear's absurdist, extravagant yet melancholy-tinged vision has inspired countless imitators.

SELF-PORTRAIT OF THE
LAUREATE OF NONSENSE

How pleasant to know Mr Lear!
Who has written such volumes of stuff!
Some think him ill-tempered and queer,
But a few find him pleasant enough.

His mind is concrete and fastidious,
His nose is remarkably big;
His visage is more or less hideous,
His beard it resembles a wig.

He has ears, and two eyes, and ten fingers,
(Leastways if you reckon two thumbs);
He used to be one of the singers,
But now he is one of the dumbs.

He sits in a beautiful parlour,
With hundreds of books on the wall;
He drinks a great deal of marsala,
But never gets tipsy at all.

He has many friends, laymen and clerical;
Old Foss is the name of his cat;
His body is perfectly spherical,
He weareth a runcible hat.

When he walks in waterproof white,
The children run after him so!
Calling out, "He's gone out in his night-
Gown, that crazy old Englishman, oh!"

He weeps by the side of the ocean,
He weeps on the top of the hill;
He purchases pancakes and lotion,
And chocolate shrimps from the mill.

He reads but he cannot speak Spanish,
He cannot abide ginger beer:
Ere the days of his pilgrimage vanish,
How pleasant to know Mr Lear!

LIMERICKS

from *A Book of Nonsense* (1846)

There was an Old Man with a beard,
Who said, "It is just as I feared!
Two Owls and a Hen,
Four Larks and a Wren,
Have all built their nests in my beard!"

* * * * *

There was a Young Person of Smyrna,
Whose Grandmother threatened to burn her;
But she seized on the cat,
And said, "Granny, burn that!
You incongruous Old Woman of Smyrna!"

* * * * *

There was a Young Lady whose chin,
Resembled the point of a pin;
So she had it made sharp,
And purchased a harp,
And played several tunes with her chin.

There was an Old Man in a boat,
Who said, "I'm afloat, I'm afloat!"
When they said, "No! you ain't!"
He was ready to faint,
That unhappy Old Man in a boat.

* * * * *

There was an Old Man of Moldavia,
Who had the most curious behaviour;
For while he was able,
He slept on a table.
That funny Old Man of Moldavia.

* * * * *

There was an Old Man of the West,
Who wore a pale plum-coloured vest;
When they said, "Does it fit?"
He replied, "Not a bit!"
That uneasy Old Man of the West.

* * * * *

There was an Old Person of Rhodes,
Who strongly objected to toads;
He paid several cousins,
To catch them by dozens,
That futile Old Person of Rhodes.

There was an Old Person of Troy,
Whose drink was warm brandy and soy;
Which he took with a spoon,
By the light of the moon,
In sight of the city of Troy.

* * * * *

There was an Old Man of Whitehaven,
Who danced a quadrille with a raven;
But they said, "It's absurd
To encourage this bird!"
So they smashed that Old Man of Whitehaven.

* * * * *

There was an Old Person of Anerley,
Whose conduct was strange and unmannerly;
He rushed down the Strand
With a pig in each hand,
But returned in the evening to Anerley.

* * * * *

There was an Old Man who said, "Well!
Will nobody answer this bell?
I have pulled day and night,
Till my hair has grown white,
But nobody answers this bell!"

There was an Old Person from Gretna,
Who rushed down the crater of Etna;
When they said, "Is it hot?"
He replied, "No, it's not!"
That mendacious Old Person of Gretna.

* * * * *

There was an Old Person of Burton,
Whose answers were rather uncertain;
When they said, "How d'ye do?"
He replied, "Who are you?"
That distressing Old Person of Burton.

* * * * *

There was an Old Person of Ems,
Who casually fell in the Thames;
And when he was found
They said he was drowned,
That unlucky Old Person of Ems.

* * * * *

There was an Old Person of Ewell,
Who chiefly subsisted on gruel;
But to make it more nice
He inserted some mice,
Which refreshed that Old Person of Ewell.

THE OWL AND THE PUSSY-CAT

The Owl and the Pussy-cat went to sea
In a beautiful pea green boat,
They took some honey, and plenty of money,
Wrapped up in a five pound note.
The Owl looked up to the stars above,
And sang to a small guitar,
"O lovely Pussy! O Pussy my love,
What a beautiful Pussy you are,
    You are,
    You are!
What a beautiful Pussy you are!"

Pussy said to the Owl, "You elegant fowl!
How charmingly sweet you sing!
O let us be married! too long we have tarried:
But what shall we do for a ring?"
They sailed away, for a year and a day,
To the land where the Bong-tree grows
And there in a wood a Piggy-wig stood
With a ring at the end of his nose,
    His nose,
    His nose,
With a ring at the end of his nose.

"Dear pig, are you willing to sell for one shilling
Your ring?" Said the Piggy, "I will."

So they took it away, and were married next day
By the Turkey who lives on the hill.
They dined on mince, and slices of quince,
Which they ate with a runcible spoon;
And hand in hand, on the edge of the sand,
They danced by the light of the moon,
 The moon,
 The moon,
They danced by the light of the moon.

THE DUCK AND THE
KANGAROO

Said the Duck to the Kangaroo,
"Good gracious! how you hop!
Over the fields and the water too,
As if you never would stop!
My life is a bore in this nasty pond,
And I long to go out in the world beyond!
I wish I could hop like you!"
Said the duck to the Kangaroo.

"Please give me a ride on your back!"
Said the Duck to the Kangaroo.
"I would sit quite still, and say nothing but 'Quack',
The whole of the long day through!
And we'd go to the Dee, and the Jelly Bo Lee,
Over the land and over the sea;—
Please take me a ride! O do!"
Said the Duck to the Kangaroo.

Said the Kangaroo to the Duck,
"This requires some little reflection;
Perhaps on the whole it might bring me luck,
And there seems but one objection,
Which is, if you'll let me speak so bold,
Your feet are unpleasantly wet and cold,

And would probably give me the roo-
Matiz!" said the Kangaroo.

Said the Duck, "As I sat on the rocks,
I have thought over that completely,
And I bought four pairs of worsted socks
Which fit my web-feet neatly.
And to keep out the cold I've bought a cloak,
And every day a cigar I'll smoke,
All to follow my own dear true
Love of a Kangaroo!"

Said the Kangaroo, "I'm ready!
All in the moonlight pale;
But to balance me well, dear Duck, sit steady!
And quite at the end of my tail!"
So away they went with a hop and a bound,
And they hopped the whole world three times round;
And who so happy, O who,
As the duck and the Kangaroo?

THE DADDY LONG-LEGS AND
THE FLY

Once Mr Daddy Long-legs,
Dressed in brown and grey,
Walked about upon the sands
Upon a summer's day;
And there among the pebbles,
When the wind was rather cold,
He met with Mr Floppy Fly,
All dressed in blue and gold.
And as it was too soon to dine,
They drank some Periwinkle-wine,
And played an hour or two, or more,
At battlecock and shuttledore.

Said Mr Daddy Long-legs
To Mr Floppy Fly,
"Why do you never come to court?
I wish you'd tell me why.
All gold and shine, in dress so fine,
You'd quite delight the court.
Why do you never go at all?
I really think you ought!
And if you went, you'd see such sights!
Such rugs! Such jugs! and candle-lights!
And more than all, the King and Queen,
One in red, and one in green!"

"O Mr Daddy Long-legs,"
Said Mr Floppy Fly,
"It's true I never go to court,
And I will tell you why.
If I had six long legs like yours,
At once I'd go to court!
But oh! I can't, because my legs
Are so extremely short.
And I'm afraid the King and Queen
(One in red, and one in green)
Would say aloud, 'You are not fit,
You Fly, to come to court a bit!' "

"O Mr Daddy Long-legs,"
Said Mr Floppy Fly,
"I wish you'd sing one little song!
One mumbian melody!
You used to sing so awful well
In former days gone by,
But now you never sing at all;
I wish you'd tell me why:
For if you would, the silvery sound
Would please the shrimps and cockles round,
And all the crabs would gladly come
To hear you sing, 'Ah, hum di Hum'!"

Said Mr Daddy Long-legs,
"I can never sing again!
And if you wish, I'll tell you why,

Although it gives me pain.
For years I cannot hum a bit,
Or sing the smallest song;
And this the dreadful reason is,
My legs are grown too long!
My six long legs, all here and there,
Oppress my bosom with despair;
And if I stand, or lie, or sit,
I cannot sing one little bit!"

So Mr Daddy Long-legs
And Mr Floppy Fly
Sat down in silence by the sea,
And gazed upon the sky.
They said, "This is a dreadful thing!
The world has all gone wrong,
Since one has legs too short by half,
The other much too long!
One never more can go to court,
Because his legs have grown too short;
The other cannot sing a song,
Because his legs have grown too long!"

Then Mr Daddy Long-legs
And Mr Floppy Fly
Rushed downward to the foamy sea
With one sponge-taneous cry;
And there they found a little boat,
Whose sails were pink and grey;

And off they sailed among the waves,
Far, and far away.
They sailed across the silent main,
And reached the great Gromboolian plain;
And there they play for evermore
At battlecock and shuttledore.

THE JUMBLIES

I

They went to sea in a Sieve, they did,
In a Sieve they went to sea:
In spite of all their friends could say,
On a winter's morn, on a stormy day,
In a Sieve they went to sea!
And when the Sieve turned round and round,
And every one cried, "You'll all be drowned!"
They called aloud, "Our Sieve ain't big,
But we don't care a button! we don't care a fig!
In a Sieve we'll go to sea!"
    Far and few, far and few,
    Are the lands where the Jumblies live;
    Their heads are green, and their hands are blue,
    And they went to sea in a Sieve.

II

They sailed away in a Sieve, they did,
In a Sieve they sailed so fast,
With only a beautiful pea-green veil
Tied with a riband by way of a sail,
To a small tobacco-pipe mast;
And every one said, who saw them go,
"O won't they be soon upset, you know!
For the sky is dark, and the voyage is long,

And happen what may, it's extremely wrong
In a Sieve to sail so fast!"
    Far and few, far and few,
    Are the lands where the Jumblies live;
    Their heads are green, and their hands are blue,
    And they went to sea in a Sieve.

III

The water it soon came in, it did,
The water it soon came in;
So to keep them dry, they wrapped their feet
In a pinky paper all folded neat,
And they fastened it down with a pin.
And they passed the night in a crockery-jar,
And each of them said, "How wise we are!
Though the sky be dark, and the voyage be long,
Yet we never can think we were rash or wrong,
While round in our Sieve we spin!"
    Far and few, far and few,
    Are the lands where the Jumblies live;
    Their heads are green, and their hands are blue,
    And they went to sea in a Sieve.

IV

And all night long they sailed away;
And when the sun went down,

They whistled and warbled a moony song
To the echoing sound of a coppery gong,
In the shade of the mountains brown.
"O Timballo! How happy we are,
When we live in a Sieve and a crockery-jar,
And all night long in the moonlight pale,
We sail away with a pea-green sail,
In the shade of the mountains brown!"
 Far and few, far and few,
 Are the lands where the Jumblies live;
 Their heads are green, and their hands are blue,
 And they went to sea in a Sieve.

V

They sailed to the Western Sea, they did,
To a land all covered with trees,
And they bought an Owl, and a useful Cart,
And a pound of Rice, and a Cranberry Tart,
And a hive of silvery Bees.
And they bought a Pig, and some green Jack-daws,
And a lovely Monkey with lollipop paws,
And forty bottles of Ring-Bo-Ree,
And no end of Stilton Cheese.
 Far and few, far and few,
 Are the lands where the Jumblies live;
 Their heads are green, and their hands are blue,
 And they went to sea in a Sieve.

And in twenty years they all came back,
In twenty years or more,
And every one said, "How tall they've grown!
For they've been to the Lakes, and the Torrible Zone,
And the hills of the Chankly Bore!"
And they drank their health, and gave them a feast
Of dumplings made of beautiful yeast;
And every one said, "If we only live,
We too will go to sea in a Sieve,—
To the hills of the Chankly Bore!"
    Far and few, far and few,
    Are the lands where the Jumblies live;
    Their heads are green, and their hands are blue,
    And they went to sea in a Sieve.

CALICO PIE

Calico Pie,
　The little Birds fly
Down to the calico tree,
　Their wings were blue,
　And they sang 'Tilly-loo!'
　Till away they flew,
And they never came back to me!
　They never came back!
　They never came back!
They never came back to me!

Calico Jam,
　The little Fish swam,
Over the syllabub sea,
　He took off his hat,
　To the Sole and the Sprat,
　And the Willeby-Wat,
But he never came back to me!
　He never came back!
　He never came back!
He never came back to me!

Calico Ban,
　The little Mice ran,
To be ready in time for tea,
　Flippity flup,

They drank it all up,
And danced in the cup,
But they never came back to me!
They never came back!
They never came back!
They never came back to me!

Calico Drum,
The Grasshoppers come,
The Butterfly, Beetle, and Bee,
Over the ground,
Around and around,
With a hop and a bound,
But they never came back to me!
They never came back!
They never came back!
They never came back to me!

MORE LIMERICKS

from *More Nonsense Pictures, Rhymes, Botany, etc.* (1872)

There was an Old Man of Hong Kong,
Who never did anything wrong;
He lay on his back,
With his head in a sack,
That innocuous Old Man of Hong Kong.

*****

There was an Old Person of Fife,
Who was greatly disgusted with life;
They sang him a ballad,
And fed him on salad,
Which cured that Old Person of Fife.

*****

There was an Old Person of Putney,
Whose food was roast spiders and chutney,
Which he took with his tea,
Within sight of the sea,
That romantic Old Person of Putney.

There was an Old Person of Wick,
Who said, "Tick-a-Tick, Tick-a-Tick;
Chickabee, Chickabaw,"
And he said nothing more,
That laconic Old Person of Wick.

*****

There was an Old Man of Toulouse
Who purchased a new pair of shoes;
When they asked, "Are they pleasant?"
He said, "Not at present!"
That turbid Old Man of Toulouse.

*****

There was an Old Man of Blackheath,
Whose head was adorned with a wreath
Of lobsters and spice,
Pickled onions and mice,
That uncommon Old Man of Blackheath.

*****

There was an Old Man who screamed out
Whenever they knocked him about;
So they took off his boots,
And fed him with fruits,
And continued to knock him about.

There was an Old Person of Woking,
Whose mind was perverse and provoking;
He sat on a rail,
With his head in a pail,
That illusive Old Person of Woking.

* * * * *

There was an Old Person of Shoreham,
Whose habits were marked by decorum;
He bought an Umbrella,
And sat in the cellar,
Which pleases all the people of Shoreham.

* * * * *

There was an Old Person of Skye,
Who waltz'd with a Bluebottle fly:
They buzz'd a sweet tune,
To the light of the moon,
And entranced all the people of Skye.

* * * * *

There was an Old Person of Bray,
Who sang through the whole of the day
To his ducks and his pigs,
Whom he fed upon figs,
That valuable person of Bray.

There was an Old Man of Thermopylæ,
Who never did anything propersly;
But they said, "If you choose,
To boil eggs in your shoes,
You shall never remain in Thermopylæ."

*****

There was an Old Man on the Border,
Who lived in the utmost disorder;
He danced with the cat,
And made tea in his hat,
Which vexed all the folks on the Border.

THE DONG WITH THE LUMINOUS NOSE

When awful darkness and silence reign
Over the great Gromboolian plain,
Through the long, long wintry nights;
When the angry breakers roar
As they beat on the rocky shore;
When Storm-clouds brood on the towering heights
Of the Hills of the Chankly Bore:

Then, through the vast and gloomy dark,
There moves what seems a fiery spark,
A lonely spark with silvery rays
Piercing the coal-black night,
A Meteor strange and bright:
Hither and thither the vision strays,
A single lurid light.

Slowly it wanders, pauses, creeeps,
Anon it sparkles, flashes and leaps;
And ever as onward it gleaming goes
A light on the Bong-tree stems it throws.
And those who watch at that midnight hour
From Hall or Terrace, or lofty Tower,
Cry, as the wild light passes along,
"The Dong! the Dong!
The wandering Dong through the forest goes!

The Dong! the Dong!
The Dong with a luminous Nose!"

Long years ago
The Dong was happy and gay,
Till he fell in love with a Jumbly Girl
Who came to those shores one day,
For the Jumblies came in a sieve, they did,
Landing at eve near the Zemmery Fidd
Where the Oblong Oysters grow,
And the rocks are smooth and grey.
And all the woods and the valleys rang
With the Chorus they daily and nightly sang,
  "Far and few, far and few,
  Are the lands where the Jumblies live;
  Their heads are green, and their hands are blue
  And they went to sea in a sieve."

Happily, happily passed those days!
While the cheerful Jumblies staid;
They danced in circlets all night long,
To the plaintive pipe of the lively Dong,
In moonlight, shine, or shade.
For day and night he was always there
By the side of the Jumbly Girl so fair,
With her sky-blue hands, and her sea-green hair.
Till the morning came of that hateful day
When the Jumblies sailed in their sieve away,
And the Dong was left on the cruel shore

Gazing—gazing for evermore,
Ever keeping his weary eyes on
That pea-green sail on the far horizon,
Singing the Jumbly Chorus still
As he sat all day on the grassy hill,

"Far and few, far and few,
Are the lands where the Jumblies live;
Their heads are green, and their hands are blue
And they went to sea in a sieve."

But when the sun was low in the West,
The Dong arose and said,
"What little sense I once possessed
Has quite gone out of my head!"
And since that day he wanders still
By lake or forest, marsh and hill,
Singing—"O somewhere, in valley or plain
Might I find my Jumbly Girl again!
For ever I'll seek by lake and shore
Till I find my Jumbly Girl once more!"

Playing a pipe with silvery squeaks,
Since then his Jumbly Girl he seeks,
And because by night he could not see,
He gathered the bark of the Twangum Tree
On the flowery plain that grows.
And he wove him a wondrous Nose,
A Nose as strange as a Nose could be!
Of vast proportions and painted red,

And tied with cords to the back of his head.
In a hollow rounded space it ended
With a luminous Lamp within suspended,
All fenced about
With a bandage stout
To prevent the wind from blowing it out;
And with holes all round to send the light,
In gleaming rays on the dismal night.

And now each night, and all night long,
Over those plains still roams the Dong;
And above the wall of the Chimp and Snipe
You may hear the sqeak of his plaintive pipe
While ever he seeks, but seeks in vain
To meet with his Jumbly Girl again;
Lonely and wild—all night he goes,
The Dong with a luminous Nose!
And all who watch at the midnight hour,
From Hall or Terrace, or lofty Tower,
Cry, as they trace the Meteor bright,
Moving along through the dreary night,
"This is the hour when forth he goes,
The Dong with a luminous Nose!
Yonder—over the plain he goes,
    He goes!
    He goes;
The Dong with a luminous Nose!"

THE TWO OLD BACHELORS

Two old Bachelors were living in one house;
One caught a Muffin, the other caught a Mouse.
Said he who caught the Muffin to him who caught
    the Mouse,
"This happens just in time! For we've nothing in the
    house,
Save a tiny slice of lemon nd a teaspoonful of honey,
And what to do for dinner—since we haven't any
    money?
And what can we expect if we haven't any dinner,
But to loose our teeth and eyelashes and keep on
    growing thinner?"

Said he who caught the Mouse to him who caught
    the Muffin,
"We might cook this little Mouse, if we had only
    some Stuffin'!
If we had but Sage and Onion we could do extremely
    well,
But how to get that Stuffin' it is difficult to tell"—

Those two old Bachelors ran quickly to the town
And asked for Sage and Onions as they wandered up
    and down;
They borrowed two large Onions, but no Sage was to
    be found

In the Shops, or in the Market, or in all the Gardens round.

But someone said, "A hill there is, a little to the north,
And to its purpledicular top a narrow way leads forth;
And there among the rugged rocks abides an ancient Sage,
An earnest Man, who reads all day a most perplexing page.
Climb up, and seize him by the toes! —all studious as he sits—
And pull him down, and chop him into endless little bits!
Then mix him with your Onion, (cut up likewise into Scraps)
When your Stuffin' will be ready—and very good: perhaps."

Those two old Bachelors without loss of time
The nearly purpledicular crags at once began to climb;
And at the top, among the rocks, all seated in a nook,
They saw that Sage, a reading of a most enormous book.

"You earnest Sage!" aloud they cried, "your book you've read enough in!
We wish to chop you into bits to mix you into Stuffin'!"

But that old Sage looked calmly up, and with his
    awful book,
At those two Bachelors' bald heads a certain aim he
    took;
And over crag and precipice they rolled promiscuous
    down,
At once they rolled, and never stopped in lane or field
    or town,
And when they reached their house, they found
    (besides their want of Stuffin')
The Mouse had fled; and, previously, had eaten up
    the Muffin.

They left their home in silence by the once convivial
    door.
And from that hour those Bachelors were never heard
    of more.

THE COURTSHIP OF THE YONGHY-BONGHY-BÒ

I

On the Coast of Coromandel
Where the early pumpkins blow,
In the middle of the woods
Lived the Yonghy-Bonghy-Bò.
Two old chairs, and half a candle,
One old jug without a handle,
These were all his worldly goods:
In the middle of the woods,
These were all the worldly goods
Of the Yonghy-Bonghy-Bò,
Of the Yonghy-Bonghy-Bò.

II

Once, among the Bong-trees walking
Where the early pumpkins blow,
To a little heap of stones
Came the Yonghy-Bonghy-Bò.
There he heard a Lady talking,
To some milk-white Hens of Dorking,
" 'Tis the Lady Jingly Jones!
On that little heap of stones
Sits the Lady Jingly Jones!"
Said the Yonghy-Bonghy-Bò,
Said the Yonghy-Bonghy-Bò.

III

"Lady Jingly! Lady Jingly!
Sitting where the pumpkins blow,
Will you come and be my wife?"
Said the Yonghy-Bonghy-Bò,
"I am tired of living singly,
On this coast so wild and shingly,
I'm a-weary of my life;
If you'll come and be my wife,
Quite serene would be my life!"
Said the Yonghy-Bonghy-Bò,
Said the Yonghy-Bonghy-Bò.

IV

"On this Coast of Coromandel
Shrimps and watercresses grow,
Prawns are plentiful and cheap,"
Said the Yonghy-Bonghy-Bò.
"You shall have my chairs and candle,
And my jug without a handle!
Gaze upon the rolling deep
(Fish is plentiful and cheap):
As the sea, my love is deep!"
Said the Yonghy-Bonghy-Bò,
Said the Yonghy-Bonghy-Bò.

V

Lady Jingly answered sadly,
And her tears began to flow,
"Your proposal comes too late,
Mr Yonghy-Bonghy-Bò!
I would be your wife most gladly!"
(Here she twirled her fingers madly)
"But in England I've a mate!
Yes! you've asked me far too late,
For in England I've a mate,
Mr Yonghy-Bonghy-Bò!
Mr Yonghy-Bonghy-Bò!

VI

"Mr Jones (his name is Handel—
Handel Jones, Esquire & Co.)
Dorking fowls delights to send,
Mr Yonghy-Bonghy-Bò!
Keep, oh, keep your chairs and candle,
And your jug without a handle,
I can merely be your friend!
Should my Jones more Dorkings send,
I will give you three, my friend!
Mr Yonghy-Bonghy-Bò!
Mr Yonghy-Bonghy-Bò!

VII

"Though you've such a tiny body,
And your head so large doth grow,
Though your hat may blow away,
Mr Yonghy-Bonghy-Bò!
Though you're such a Hoddy Doddy,
Yet I wish that I could modi-
-fy the words I needs must say!
Will you please to go away?
That is all I have to say,
Mr Yonghy-Bonghy-Bò!
Mr Yonghy-Bonghy-Bò!"

VIII

Down the slippery slopes of Myrtle,
Where the early pumpkins blow,
To the calm and silent sea
Fled the Yonghy-Bonghy-Bò.
There, beyond the Bay of Gurtle,
Lay a large and lively Turtle.
"You're the Cove," he said, "for me:
On your back beyond the sea,
Turtle, you shall carry me!"
Said the Yonghy-Bonghy-Bò,
Said the Yonghy-Bonghy-Bò.

IX

Through the silent roaring ocean
Did the Turtle swiftly go;
Holding fast upon his shell
Rode the Yonghy-Bonghy-Bò.
With a sad primeval motion
Toward the sunset isles of Boshen
Still the Turtle bore him well,
Holding fast upon his shell.
"Lady Jingly Jones, farewell!"
Sang the Yonghy-Bonghy-Bò,
Sang the Yonghy-Bonghy-Bò.

X

From the Coast of Coromandel
Did that Lady never go,
On that heap of stones she mourns
For the Yonghy-Bonghy-Bò.
On that Coast of Coromandel,
In his jug without a handle
Still she weeps, and daily moans;
On that little heap of stones
To her Dorking Hens she moans,
For the Yonghy-Bonghy-Bò,
For the Yonghy-Bonghy-Bò.

THE POBBLE WHO HAS NO TOES

The Pobble who has no toes
Had once as many as we;
When they said, "Some day you may lose them all;"
He replied, "Fish, fiddle-de-dee!"
And his Aunt Jobiska made him drink
Lavender water tinged with pink,
For she said, "The World in general knows
There's nothing so good for a Pobble's toes!"

The Pobble who has no toes
Swam across the Bristol Channel;
But before he set out he wrapped his nose
In a piece of scarlet flannel.
For his Aunt Jobiska said, "No harm
Can come to his toes if his nose is warm;
And it's perfectly known that a Pobble's toes
Are safe, provided he minds his nose!"

The Pobble swam fast and well,
And when boats or ships came near him,
He tinkledy-blinkledy-winkled a bell,
So that all the world could hear him.
And all the Sailors and Admirals cried,
When they saw him nearing the further side—
"He has gone to fish for his Aunt Jobiska's
Runcible Cat with crimson whiskers!"

But before he touched the shore,
The shore of the Bristol Channel,
A sea-green porpoise carried away
His wrapper of scarlet flannel.
And when he came to observe his feet,
Formerly garnished with toes so neat,
His face at once became forlorn,
On perceiving that all his toes were gone!

And nobody ever knew,
From that dark day to the present,
Whoso had taken the Pobble's toes,
In a manner so far from pleasant.
Whether the shrimps, or crawfish grey,
Or crafty Mermaids stole them away—
Nobody knew: and nobody knows
How the Pobble was robbed of his twice five toes!

The Pobble who has no toes
Was placed in a friendly Bark,
And they rowed him back, and carried him up
To his Aunt Jobiska's Park.
And she made him a feast at his earnest wish
Of eggs and buttercups fried with fish,
And she said, "It's a fact the whole world knows,
That Pobbles are happier without their toes!"

THE NEW VESTMENTS

There lived an old man in the kingdom of Tess,
Who invented a purely original dress;
And when it was perfectly made and complete,
He opened the door, and walked into the street.

By way of a hat, he'd a loaf of Brown Bread,
In the middle of which he inserted his head;
His Shirt was made up of no end of dead Mice,
The warmth of whose skins was quite fluffy and nice;
His Drawers were of Rabbit-skins, so were his Shoes;
His stockings were skins, but it is not known whose;
His Waistcoat and Trousers were made of Pork Chops;
His Buttons were Jujubes, and Chocolate Drops;
His Coat was all Pancakes with Jam for a border,
And a girdle of Biscuits to keep it in order;
And he wore over all, as a screen from bad weather,
A Cloak of green Cabbage-leaves stitched all together.

He had walked a short way, when he heard a great
    noise,
Of all sorts of Beasticles, Birdlings, and Boys;
And from every long street and dark lane in the town
Beasts, Birdies, and Boys in a tumult rushed down.
Two Cows and a half ate his Cabbage-leaf Cloak;
Four Apes seized his Girdle, which vanished like
    smoke;

Three Kids ate up half of his Pancaky Coat,
And the tails were devour'd by an ancient He-Goat;
An army of Dogs in a twinkling tore up his
Pork Waistcoat and Trousers to give to their Puppies;
And while they were growling, and mumbling the
　　Chops,
Ten boys prigged the Jujubes and Chocolate Drops.
He tried to run back to his house, but in vain,
Four Scores of fat Pigs came again and again;
They rushed out of stables and hovels and doors,
They tore off his stockings, his shoes, and his drawers;
And now from the housetops with screechings
　　descend,
Striped, spotted, white, black, and grey Cats without
　　end,
They jumped on his shoulders and knocked off his
　　hat,
When Crows, Ducks, and Hens made a mincemeat of
　　that;
They speedily flew at his sleeves in trice,
And utterly tore up his Shirt of dead Mice;
They swallowed the last of his Shirt with a squall,
Whereon he ran home with no clothes on at all.

And he said to himself as he bolted the door,
"I will not wear a similar dress any more,
Any more, any more, any more, never more!"

THE QUANGLE WANGLE'S HAT

On the top of the Crumpetty Tree
The Quangle Wangle sat,
But his face you could not see,
On account of his Beaver Hat.
For his hat was a hundred and two feet wide,
With ribbons and bibbons on every side
And bells, and buttons, and loops, and lace,
So that nobody ever could see the face
Of the Quangle Wangle Quee.

The Quangle Wangle said
To himself on the Crumpetty Tree,
"Jam; and jelly; and bread;
Are the best food for me!
But the longer I live on this Crumpetty Tree
The plainer than ever it seems to me
That very few people come this way
And that life on the whole is far from gay!"
Said the Quangle Wangle Quee.

But there came to the Crumpetty Tree,
Mr and Mrs Canary;
And they said, "Did you ever see
Any spot so charmingly airy?
May we build a nest on your lovely Hat?
Mr Quangle Wangle, grant us that!

O please let us come and build a nest
Of whatever material suits you best,
Mr Quangle Wangle Quee!"

And besides, to the Crumpetty Tree
Came the Stork, the Duck, and the Owl;
The Snail, and the Bumble-Bee,
The Frog, and the Fimble Fowl;
The Fimble Fowl, with a Corkscrew leg;
And all of them said, "We humbly beg,
We may build our homes on your lovely Hat,
Mr Quangle Wangle, grant us that!
Mr Quangle Wangle Quee!"

And the Golden Grouse came there,
And the Pobble who has no toes,
And the small Olympian bear,
And the Dong with a luminous nose.
And the Blue Baboon, who played the flute,
And the Orient Calf from the Land of Tute,
And the Attery Squash, and the Bisky Bat,
All came and built on the lovely Hat
Of the Quangle Wangle Quee.

And the Quangle Wangle said
To himself on the Crumpetty Tree,
"When all these creatures move
What a wonderful noise there'll be!"
And at night by the light of the Mulberry moon

They danced to the flute of the Blue Baboon,
On the broad green leaves of the Crumpetty Tree,
And all were as happy as happy could be,
With the Quangle Wangle Quee.

THE CUMMERBUND

An Indian Poem

She sat upon her Dobie,
To watch the Evening Star,
And all the Punkahs as they passed,
Cried, "My! how fair you are!"
Around her bower, with quivering leaves,
The tall Kamsamahs grew,
And Kitmutgars in wild festoons
Hung down from Tchokis blue.

Below her home the river rolled
With soft meloobious sound,
Where golden-finned Chuprassies swam,
In myriads circling round.
Above, on talles trees remote
Green Ayahs perched alone,
And all night long the Mussak moan'd
Its melancholy tone.

And where the purple Nullahs threw
Their branches far and wide,
And silvery Goreewallahs flew
In silence, side by side,
The little Bheesties' twittering cry
Rose on the fragrant air,

And oft the angry Jampan howled
Deep in his hateful lair.

She sat upon her Dobie,
She heard the Nimmak hum,
When all at once a cry arose,
"The Cummerbund is come!"
In vain she fled: with open jaws
The angry monster followed,
And so (before assistance came)
That Lady Fair was swallowed.

They sought in vain for even a bone
Respectfully to bury,
They said, "Hers was a dreadful fate!"
(And Echo answered "Very.")
They nailed her Dobie to the wall,
Where last her form was seen,
And underneath they wrote these words,
In yellow, blue, and green:
'Beware, ye Fair! Ye Fair, beware!
Nor sit out late at night,
Lest horrid Cummerbunds should come,
And swallow you outright.'

THE AKOND OF SWAT

Who, or why, or which, or *what*,
    Is the Akond of Swat?

Is he tall or short, or dark or fair?
Does he sit on a stool or sofa or chair,
    Or *squat*,
    The Akond of Swat?

Is he wise or foolish, young or old?
Does he drink his soup and his coffee cold,
    Or *hot*,
    The Akond of Swat?

Does he sing or whistle, jabber or talk,
And when riding abroad does he gallop or walk,
    Or *trot*,
    The Akond of Swat?

Does he wear a turban, a fez or a hat?
Does he sleep on a mattress, a bed or a mat,
    Or a *cot*,
    The Akond of Swat?

When he writes a copy in round-hand size,
Does he cross his t's and finish his i's
    With a *dot*,
    The Akond of Swat?

Can he write a letter concisely clear,
Without a speck or a smudge or smear
    Or *blot*,
    The Akond of Swat?

Do his people like him extremely well?
Or do they, whenever they can, rebel,
    Or *plot*,
    At the Akond of Swat?

If he catches them then, either old or young,
Does he have them chopped in pieces or hung,
    Or *shot*,
    The Akond of Swat?

Do his people prig in the lanes or park?
Or even at times, when days are dark,
    Garotte?
    O the Akond of Swat?

Does he study the wants of his own dominion?
Or doesn't he care for public opinion,
    A *jot*,
    The Akond of Swat?

To amuse his mind do his people show him
Pictures, or any one's last new poem,
    Or *what*,
    For the Akond of Swat?

At night if he suddenly screams and wakes,
Do they bring him only a few small cakes,
>   Or a *lot*,
>   For the Akond of Swat?

Does he live on turnips, tea or tripe,
Does he like his shawl to be marked with a stripe,
>   Or a *dot*,
>   The Akond of Swat?

Does he like to lie on his back in a boat
Like the lady who lived in that isle remote,
>   *Shalott*,
>   The Akond of Swat?

Is he quiet, or always making a fuss?
Is his steward a Swiss or a Swede or a Russ,
>   Or a *Scot*,
>   The Akond of Swat?

Does he like to sit by the calm blue wave?
Or to sleep and snore in a dark green cave,
>   Or a *grott*,
>   The Akond of Swat?

Does he drink small beer from a silver jug?
Or a bowl? or a glass? or a cup? or a mug?
>   Or a *pot*,
>   The Akond of Swat?

Does he beat his wife with a gold-topped pipe,
When she lets the gooseberries grow too ripe,
    Or *rot*,
    The Akond of Swat?

Does he wear a white tie when he dines with his
    friends,
And tie it neat in a bow with ends,
    Or a *knot*,
    The Akond of Swat?

Does he like new cream, and hate mince-pies?
When he looks at the sun does he wink his eyes,
    Or *not*,
    The Akond of Swat?

Does he teach his subjects to roast and bake?
Does he sail about on an inland lake,
    In a *yacht*,
    The Akond of Swat?

Some one, or nobody knows I wot
Who or which or why or what
    Is the Akond of Swat!

INCIDENTS IN THE LIFE OF MY UNCLE ARLY

I

O my aged Uncle Arly!
Sitting on a heap of Barley
Thro' the silent hours of night,
Close beside a leafy thicket:
On his nose there was a Cricket,
In his hat a Railway-Ticket
(But his shoes were far too tight).

II

Long ago, in youth, he squander'd
All his goods away, and wander'd
To the Tiniskoop-hills afar.
There on golden sunsets blazing,
Every morning found him gazing,
Singing "Orb! you're quite amazing!
How I wonder what you are!"

III

Like the ancient Medes and Persians,
Always by his own exertions
He subsisted on those hills;

Whiles, by teaching children spelling,
Or at times by merely yelling,
Or at intervals by selling
'Propter's Nicodemus Pills'.

IV

Later, in his morning rambles
He perceived the moving brambles
Something square and white disclose;
'Twas a First-class Railway Ticket;
But, on stooping down to pick it
Off the ground, a pea-green Cricket
Settled on my uncle's Nose.

V

Never—never more—Oh! never,
Did that Cricket leave him ever,
Dawn or evening, day or night;
Clinging as a constant treasure,
Chirping with a cheerious measure,
Wholly to my uncle's pleasure
(Though his shoes were far too tight).

VI

So for three-and-forty winters,
Till his shoes were worn to splinters,

All those hills he wander'd o'er,
Sometimes silent; sometimes yelling;
Till he came to Borley-Melling,
Near his old ancestral dwelling
(But his shoes were far too tight).

VII

On a little heap of Barley
Died my aged uncle Arly,
And they buried him one night;
Close beside the leafy thicket;
There, his hat and Railway-Ticket;
There, his ever-faithful Cricket
(But his shoes were far too tight).

LEWIS CARROLL
(1832–1898)

Like Edward Lear, the pseudonymous Lewis Carroll (real name Charles Lutwidge Dodgson) was a man of many talents. His entire career was spent at the University of Oxford as an academic studying pure mathematics and logic, and he published a number of worthwhile – though not groundbreaking – treatises on the subjects. Like Lear, he had an instinct towards illustration, though in his case he quickly realised that he lacked the natural aptitude necessary for any great success. He turned instead to the new science of photography: before he was an author he was well known as Britain's leading photographer of children.

It was his natural rapport with children that led to Dodgson's most celebrated works, the fantastical prose and poems which were published in *Alice in Wonderland*, *Through the Looking Glass*, *Phantasmagoria* and *The Hunting of the Snark*, among others. These he published under the name Lewis Carroll (based on a transposition of his first two initials) in order to keep them distinct from his own scholarly writings.

The foundations of Lewis Carroll's vision were laid early. Born in 1832 in Cheshire, he was a precocious child and was soon regaling his brothers and sisters with humorous poems and stories, producing his first collection, *Useful and Instructive Poetry*, at the age of 13. In this, as in other early writings, can be seen the first glimmers of poems and characters that would be fully fleshed out in the pages of *Alice in Wonderland* and its sequel.

Carroll's broad education and his love of games and puzzles are evident throughout his work. The classic nonsense-rhyme 'Jabberwocky' was based on a parody of Anglo-Saxon epic poetry, and many of his verses derive from distortions of poems he would have learnt in the schoolroom. Others, such as 'A Boat Beneath a Sunny Sky' are acrostics (in this case the first letters of each line spell out the name of Alice Liddell, Carroll's youthful muse). Famously, *Through the Looking Glass* constitutes, in story form, a chess puzzle which Carroll set out at the start of the work – '*White Pawn (Alice) to play, and win in eleven moves*'. Alice's journey through the looking-glass world, and the characters she meets, correspond precisely to her piece's passage across the board.

Carroll's last great nonsense creation, *The Hunting of the Snark* (1876), represents the longest, most fully-rounded nonsense work in the English language. Borrowing much of its detail from 'Jabberwocky', it bears comparison with Coleridge's *The Rime of the Ancient Mariner* as well as Homer's *Odyssey*. In the years around and following its publication, Carroll spend two decades drawing together the strands of the rambling, disappointing *Sylvie and Bruno* (1889–93). Even here, there were nuggets of genius to be found, and in 'The Mad Gardener's Song', Carroll created both a truly memorable poem and an original verse form (since christened the 'Waterford' as an alternative to the 'Limerick').

Carroll's legacy is the enduring world of Alice and the volume of words and phrases he has contributed to the English vocabulary. From his original coinings of 'chortle' and 'galumph' to the White Queen's maxim of 'Jam tomorrow and jam yesterday – but never jam today', Carroll has achieved that rare status achieved by the Bible or Shakespeare: he is quoted on a daily basis, often without people realising they are doing so.

THE MOUSE'S TAIL

Fury said to a mouse,
That he met in the
house, "Let us
both go to law:
I will prosecute
you.—Come, I'll
take no denial:
We must have
the trial; For
really this
morning I've
nothing to do."
Said the mouse
to the cur,
"Such a trial,
dear Sir, With
no jury or
judge, would
be wasting
our breath."
"I'll   be
judge, I'll
be jury,"
Said cun-
ning old
Fury: "I'll
try the
whole
cause,
and
con-
demn
you to
death."

FATHER WILLIAM

"You are old, Father William," the young man said,
"And your hair has become very white;
And yet you incessantly stand on your head—
Do you think, at your age, it is right?"

"In my youth," Father William replied to his son,
"I feared it might injure the brain;
But, now that I'm perfectly sure I have none,
Why, I do it again and again."

"You are old," said the youth, "as I mentioned before,
And have grown most uncommonly fat;
Yet you turned a back-somersault in at the door—
Pray, what is the reason of that?"

"In my youth," said the sage, as he shook his grey
    locks,
"I kept all my limbs very supple
By the use of this ointment — one shilling the box —
Allow me to sell you a couple?"

"You are old," said the youth, "and your jaws are too
    weak
For anything tougher than suet;

Yet you finished the goose, with the bones and the
    beak—
Pray, how did you manage to do it?"

"In my youth," said his father, "I took to the law,
And argued each case with my wife;
And the muscular strength which it gave to my jaw
Has lasted the rest of my life."

"You are old," said the youth, "one would hardly
    suppose
That your eye was as steady as ever;
Yet you balanced an eel on the end of your nose—
What made you so awfully clever?"

"I have answered three questions, and that is
    enough,"
Said his father; "don't give yourself airs!
Do you think I can listen all day to such stuff?
Be off, or I'll kick you down-stairs!"

THE LOBSTER QUADRILLE

"Will you walk a little faster?" said a whiting to a
　　snail,
"There's a porpoise close behind us, and he's
　　treading on my tail.
See how eagerly the lobsters and the turtles all
　　advance!
They are waiting on the shingle—will you come and
　　join the dance?
Will you, won't you, will you, won't you, will you join
　　the dance?
Will you, won't you, will you, won't you, won't you
　　join the dance?

"You can really have no notion how delightful it will
　　be
When they take us up and throw us, with the lobsters,
　　out to sea!"
But the snail replied "Too far, too far!" and gave a
　　look askance—
Said he thanked the whiting kindly, but he would not
　　join the dance.
Would not, could not, would not, could not, would
　　not join the dance.
Would not, could not, would not, could not, could
　　not join the dance.

"What matters it how far we go?" his scaly friend
   replied.
"There is another shore, you know, upon the other
   side.
The further off from England the nearer is to
   France—
Then turn not pale, beloved snail, but come and join
   the dance.
Will you, won't you, will you, won't you, will you join
   the dance?
Will you, won't you, will you, won't you, won't you
   join the dance?"

THE WHITE RABBIT'S VERSES

They told me you had been to her,
  And mentioned me to him;
  She gave me a good character,
  But said I could not swim.

He sent them word I had not gone.
  (We know it to be true.)
  If she should push the matter on,
  What would become of you?

I gave her one, they gave him two,
  You gave us three or more;
  They all returned from him to you,
  Though they were mine before.

If I or she should chance to be
  Involved in this affair,
  He trusts to you to set them free,
  Exactly as we were.

My notion was that you had been
  (Before she had this fit)
  An obstacle that came between
  Him and ourselves and it.

Don't let him know she liked them best,
  For this must ever be
  A secret, kept from all the rest,
  Between yourself and me.

A SEA DIRGE

There are certain things—as, a spider, a ghost,
The income tax, gout, an umbrella for three—
That I hate, but the thing that I hate the most
Is a thing they call the Sea.

Pour some salt water over the floor—
Ugly I'm sure you'll allow it to be:
Suppose it extended a mile or more,
That's very like the Sea.

Beat a dog till it howls outright—
Cruel, but all very well for a spree:
Suppose that he did so day and night,
That would be like the Sea.

I had a vision of nursery-maids;
Tens of thousands passed by me—
All leading children with wooden spades,
And this was by the Sea.

Who invented those spades of wood?
Who was it cut them out of the tree?
None, I think, but an idiot could—
Or one that loved the Sea.

It is pleasant and dreamy, no doubt, to float
With 'thoughts as boundless, and souls as free':
But, suppose you are very unwell in the boat,
How do you like the Sea?

There is an insect that people avoid
(Whence is derived the verb 'to flee').
Where have you been by it most annoyed?
In lodgings by the Sea.

If you like your coffee with sand for dregs,
A decided hint of salt in your tea,
And a fishy taste in the very eggs—
By all means choose the Sea.

And if, with these dainties to drink and eat,
You prefer not a vestige of grass or tree,
And a chronic state of wet in your feet,
Then—I recommend the Sea.

For I have friends who dwell by the coast—
Pleasant friends they are to me!
It is when I am with them I wonder most
That anyone likes the Sea.

They take me a walk: though tired and stiff,
To climb the heights I madly agree;
And, after a tumble or so from the cliff,
They kindly suggest the Sea.

I try the rocks, and I think it cool
That they laugh with such an excess of glee,
As I heavily slip into every pool
That skirts the cold cold Sea.

YE CARPETTE KNYGHTE

I have a horse—a ryghte good horse—
Ne doe Y envye those
Who scoure ye playne yn headye course
Tyll soddayne on theyre nose
They lyghte wyth unexpected force
Yt ys—a horse of clothes.

I have a saddel—"Say'st thou soe?
Wyth styrruppes, Knyghte, to boote?"
I sayde not that—I answere "Noe"—
Yt lacketh such, I woote:
Yt ys a mutton-saddel, loe!
Parte of ye fleecye brute.

I have a bytte—a ryghte good bytte—
As shall bee seene yn tyme.
Ye jawe of horse yt wyll not fytte;
Yts use ys more sublyme.
Fayre Syr, how deemest thou of yt?
Yt ys—thys bytte of rhyme.

JABBERWOCKY

'Twas brillig, and the slithy toves
Did gyre and gimble in the wabe:
All mimsy were the borogoves,
And the mome raths outgrabe.

"Beware the Jabberwock, my son!
The jaws that bite, the claws that catch!
Beware the jubjub bird, and shun
The frumious Bandersnatch!"

He took his vorpal sword in hand:
Long time the manxome foe he sought—
So rested he by the Tumtum tree,
And stood awhile in thought.

And, as in uffish thought he stood,
The Jabberwock, with eyes of flame,
Came whiffling through the tulgey wood,
And burbled as it came!

One, two! One, two! And through and through
The vorpal blade went snicker-snack!
He left it dead, and with its head
He went galumphing back.

"And hast thou slain the Jabberwock?
Come to my arms, my beamish boy!
O frabjous day! Callooh! Callay!"
He chortled in his joy.

'Twas brillig, and the slithy toves
Did gyre and gimble in the wabe:
All mimsy were the borogoves,
And the mome raths outgrabe.

THE WALRUS AND THE CARPENTER

The sun was shining on the sea,
Shining with all his might;
He did his very best to make
The billows smooth and bright—
And this was odd, because it was
The middle of the night.

The moon was shining sulkily,
Because she thought the sun
Had got no business to be there
After the day was done—
"It's very rude of him,' she said,
"To come and spoil the fun!"

The sea was wet as wet could be,
The sands were dry as dry.
You could not see a cloud, because
No cloud was in the sky;
No birds were flying overhead—
There were no birds to fly.

The Walrus and the Carpenter
Were walking close at hand;
They wept like anything to see
Such quantities of sand—

"If this were only cleared away,"
They said, "it would be grand!"

"If seven maids with seven mops
Swept it for half a year,
Do you suppose," the Walrus said,
"That they could get it clear?"
"I doubt it," said the Carpenter,
And shed a bitter tear.

"O Oysters, come and walk with us!"
The Walrus did beseech.
"A pleasant walk, a pleasant talk,
Along the briny beach;
We cannot do with more than four,
To give a hand to each."

The eldest Oyster looked at him,
But never a word he said;
The eldest Oyster winked his eye,
And shook his heavy head—
Meaning to say he did not choose
To leave the oyster-bed.

But four young Oysters hurried up,
All eager for the treat;
Their coats were brushed, their faces washed,
Their shoes were clean and neat—
And this was odd, because, you know,
They hadn't any feet.

Four other Oysters followed them,
And yet another four;
And thick and fast they came at last,
And more, and more, and more—
All hopping through the frothy waves,
And scrambling to the shore.

The Walrus and the Carpenter
Walked on a mile or so,
And then they rested on a rock
Conveniently low—
And all the little Oysters stood
And waited in a row.

"The time has come," the Walrus said,
"To talk of many things:
Of shoes and ships and sealing-wax,
Of cabbages and kings,
And why the sea is boiling hot,
And whether pigs have wings."

"But wait a bit," the Oysters cried,
"Before we have our chat;
For some of us are out of breath,
And all of us are fat!"
"No hurry!" said the Carpenter.
They thanked him much for that.

"A loaf of bread," the Walrus said,
"Is what we chiefly need;

Pepper and vinegar besides
Are very good indeed—
Now, if you're ready, Oysters dear,
We can begin to feed."

"But not on us!" the Oysters cried,
Turning a little blue.
"After such kindness, that would be
A dismal thing to do!"
"The night is fine," the Walrus said.
"Do you admire the view?"

"It was so kind of you to come!
And you are very nice!"
The Carpenter said nothing but,
"Cut us another slice.
I wish you were not quite so deaf—
I've had to ask you twice!"

"It seems a shame," the Walrus said,
"To play them such a trick.
After we've brought them out so far,
And made them trot so quick!"
The Carpenter said nothing but,
"The butter's spread too thick!"

"I weep for you," the Walrus said;
"I deeply sympathize."
With sobs and tears he sorted out
Those of the largest size,

Holding his pocket-handkerchief
Before his streaming eyes.

"O Oysters," said the Carpenter,
"You've had a pleasant run!
Shall we be trotting home again?"
But answer came there none—
And this was scarcely odd, because
They'd eaten every one.

THE WHITE KNIGHT'S SONG

I'll tell thee everything I can;
There's little to relate.
I saw an aged, aged man,
A-sitting on a gate.
"Who are you, aged man?" I said.
"And how is it you live?"
And his answer trickled through my head
Like water through a sieve.

He said, "I look for butterflies
That sleep among the wheat;
I make them into mutton pies,
And sell them in the street.
I sell them unto men," he said,
"Who sail on stormy seas;
And that's the way I get my bread—
A trifle, if you please."

But I was thinking of a plan
To dye one's whiskers green,
And always use so large a fan
That they could not be seen.
So, having no reply to give
To what the old man said,
I cried, "Come, tell me how you live!"
And thumped him on the head.

His accents mild took up the tale;
He said, "I go my ways,
And when I find a mountain-rill,
I set it in a blaze;
And thence they make a stuff they call
Rowlands' Macassar Oil—
Yet twopence-halfpenny is all
They give me for my toil."

But I was thinking of a way
To feed one's self on batter,
And so go on from day to day
Getting a little fatter.
I shook him well from side to side,
Until his face was blue,
"Come, tell me how you live," I cried,
"And what it is you do!"

He said, "I hunt for haddocks' eyes
Among the heather bright,
And work them into waistcoat-buttons
In the silent night.
And these I do not sell for gold
Or coin of silvery shine,
But for a copper halfpenny,
And that will purchase nine.

"I sometimes dig for buttered rolls,
Or set limed twigs for crabs;

I sometimes search the grassy knolls
For wheels of hansom-cabs.
And that's the way" (he gave a wink)
"By which I get my wealth—
And very gladly will I drink
Your Honour's noble health."

I heard him then, for I had just
Completed my design
To keep the Menai bridge from rust
By boiling it in wine.
I thanked him much for telling me
The way he got his wealth,
But chiefly for his wish that he
Might drink my noble health.

And now, if e'er by chance I put
My fingers into glue,
Or madly squeeze a right-hand foot
Into a left-hand shoe,
Or if I drop upon my toe
A very heavy weight,
I weep, for it reminds me so
Of that old man I used to know—
Whose look was mild, whose speech was slow,
Whose hair was whiter than the snow,
Whose face was very like a crow,
With eyes, like cinders, all aglow,
Who seemed distracted with his woe,

Who rocked his body to and fro,
And muttered mumblingly and low,
As if his mouth were full of dough,
Who snorted like a buffalo—
That summer evening long ago,
A-sitting on a gate.

A BOAT BENEATH A SUNNY SKY

A boat, beneath a sunny sky,
Lingering onward dreamily
In an evening of July—

Children three that nestle near,
Eager eye and willing ear,
Pleased a simple tale to hear—

Long has paled that sunny sky;
Echoes fade and memories die;
Autumn frosts have slain July.

Still she haunts me, phantomwise,
Alice moving under skies
Never seen by waking eyes.

Children yet, the tale to hear,
Eager eye and willing ear,
Lovingly shall nestle near.

In a Wonderland they lie,
Dreaming as the days go by,
Dreaming as the summers die;

Ever drifting down the stream—
Lingering in the golden gleam—
Life, what is it but a dream?

THE MANLET

In stature the Manlet was dwarfish—
No burly, big Blunderbore he;
And he wearily gazed on the crawfish
His Wifelet had dressed for his tea.
"Now reach me, sweet Atom, my gunlet,
And hurl the old shoelet for luck;
Let me hie to the bank of the runlet,
And shoot thee a Duck!"

She has reached him his minikin gunlet;
She has hurled the old shoelet for luck;
She is busily baking a bunlet,
To welcome him home with his Duck.
On he speeds, never wasting a wordlet,
Though thoughtlets cling, closely as wax,
To the spot where the beautiful birdlet
So quietly quacks.

Where the Lobsterlet lurks, and the Crablet
So slowly and sleepily crawls;
Where the Dolphin's at home, and the Dablet
Pays long, ceremonious calls;
Where the Grublet is sought by the Froglet;
Where the Frog is pursued by the Duck;
Where the Ducklet is chased by the Doglet—
So runs the world's luck!

He has loaded with bullet and powder;
His footfall is noiseless as air;
But the Voices grow louder and louder,
And bellow and bluster and blare.
They bristle before him and after,
They flutter above and below,
Shrill shriekings of lubberly laughter,
Weird wailings of woe!

They echo without him, within him;
They thrill through his whiskers and beard;
Like a teetotum seeming to spin him,
With sneers never hitherto sneered.
"Avengement," they cry, "on our Foelet!
Let the Manikin weep for our wrongs!
Let us drench him, from toplet to toelet,
With Nursery Songs!

"He shall muse upon 'Hey! Diddle! Diddle!'
On the Cow that surmounted the Moon;
He shall rave of the Cat and the Fiddle,
And the Dish that eloped with the Spoon;
And his soul shall be sad for the Spider,
When Miss Muffet was sipping her whey,
That so tenderly sat down beside her,
And scared her away!

"The music of Midsummer madness
Shall sting him with many a bite,

Till, in rapture of rollicking sadness,
He shall groan with a gloomy delight;
He shall swathe him, like mists of the morning,
In platitudes luscious and limp,
Such as deck, with a deathless adorning,
The Song of the Shrimp!

"When the Ducklet's dark doom is decided,
We will trundle him home in a trice;
And the banquet, so plainly provided,
Shall round into rose-buds and rice;
In a blaze of pragmatic invention
He shall wrestle with Fate, and shall reign;
But he has not a friend fit to mention,
So hit him again!"

He has shot it, the delicate darling!
And the Voices have ceased from their strife;
Not a whisper of sneering or snarling,
As he carries it home to his wife;
Then, cheerily champing the bunlet
His spouse was so skilful to bake,
He hies him once more to the runlet
To fetch her the Drake!

THE MAD GARDENER'S SONG

He thought he saw an Elephant,
That practised on a fife:
He looked again, and found it was
A letter from his wife.
"At length I realise," he said,
The bitterness of Life!"

He thought he saw a Buffalo
Upon the chimney-piece:
He looked again, and found it was
His Sister's Husband's Niece.
"Unless you leave this house," he said,
"I'll send for the Police!"

He thought he saw a Rattlesnake
That questioned him in Greek:
He looked again, and found it was
The Middle of Next Week.
"The one thing I regret," he said,
"Is that it cannot speak!"

He thought he saw a Banker's Clerk
Descending from the bus:
He looked again, and found it was
A Hippopotamus.

"If this should stay to dine," he said,
"There won't be much for us!"

He thought he saw a Kangaroo
That worked a coffee mill:
He looked again, and found it was
A Vegetable Pill.
"Were I to swallow this," he said,
"I should be very ill!"

He thought he saw a Coach-and-Four
That stood beside his bed:
He looked again, and found it was
A Bear without a Head.
"Poor thing," he said, "poor silly thing!
It's waiting to be fed!"

He thought he saw an Albatross
That fluttered round the lamp:
He looked again, and found it was
A Penny Postage Stamp.
"You'd best be getting home," he said:
"The nights are very damp!"

He thought he saw a Garden Door
That opened with a key:
He looked again, and found it was
A Double Rule of Three:

"And all its mystery," he said,
"Is clear as day to me!"

He thought he saw a Argument
That proved he was the Pope:
He looked again, and found it was
A Bar of Mottled Soap.
"A fact so dread," he faintly said,
"Extinguishes all hope!"

PHANTASMAGORIA

CANTO I: *The Trystyng*

One winter night, at half-past nine,
Cold, tired, and cross, and muddy,
I had come home, too late to dine,
And supper, with cigars and wine,
Was waiting in the study.

There was a strangeness in the room,
And Something white and wavy
Was standing near me in the gloom—
I took it for the carpet-broom
Left by that careless slavey.

But presently the Thing began
To shiver and to sneeze:
On which I said "Come, come, my man!
That's a most inconsiderate plan.
Less noise there, if you please!"

"I've caught a cold," the Thing replies,
"Out there upon the landing."
I turned to look in some surprise,
And there, before my very eyes,
A little Ghost was standing!

He trembled when he caught my eye,
And got behind a chair.
"How came you here," I said, "and why?
I never saw a thing so shy.
Come out! Don't shiver there!"

He said "I'd gladly tell you how,
And also tell you why;
But" (here he gave a little bow)
"You're in so bad a temper now,
You'd think it all a lie.

"And as to being in a fright,
Allow me to remark
That Ghosts have just as good a right
In every way, to fear the light,
As Men to fear the dark."

"No plea," said I, "can well excuse
Such cowardice in you:
For Ghosts can visit when they choose,
Whereas we Humans can't refuse
To grant the interview."

He said, "A flutter of alarm
Is not unnatural, is it?
I really feared you meant some harm:
But, now I see that you are calm,
Let me explain my visit.

"Houses are classed, I beg to state,
According to the number
Of Ghosts that they accommodate:
(The Tenant merely counts as *weight*,
With Coals and other lumber).

"This is a 'one-ghost' house, and you
When you arrived last summer,
May have remarked a Spectre who
Was doing all that Ghosts can do
To welcome the new-comer.

"In Villas this is always done—
However cheaply rented:
For, though of course there's less of fun
When there is only room for one,
Ghosts have to be contented.

"That Spectre left you on the Third—
Since then you've not been haunted:
For, as he never sent us word,
'Twas quite by accident we heard
That any one was wanted.

"A Spectre has first choice, by right,
In filling up a vacancy;
Then Phantom, Goblin, Elf, and Sprite—
If all these fail them, they invite
The nicest Ghoul that they can see.

"The Spectres said the place was low,
And that you kept bad wine:
So, as a Phantom had to go,
And I was first, of course, you know,
I couldn't well decline."

"No doubt," said I, "they settled who
Was fittest to be sent;
Yet still to choose a brat like you,
To haunt a man of forty-two,
Was no great compliment!"

"I'm not so young, Sir," he replied,
"As you might think. The fact is,
In caverns by the water-side,
And other places that I've tried,
I've had a lot of practice:

"But I have never taken yet
A strict domestic part,
And in my flurry I forget
The Five Good Rules of Etiquette
We have to know by heart."

My sympathies were warming fast
Towards the little fellow:
He was so utterly aghast
At having found a Man at last,
And looked so scared and yellow.

"At least," I said, "I'm glad to find
A Ghost is not a *dumb* thing!
But pray sit down: you'll feel inclined
(If, like myself, you have not dined)
To take a snack of something:

"Though, certainly, you don't appear
A thing to offer *food* to!
And then I shall be glad to hear—
If you will say them loud and clear—
The Rules that you allude to."

"Thanks! You shall hear them by and by.
This *is* a piece of luck!"
"What may I offer you?" said I.
"Well, since you *are* so kind, I'll try
A little bit of duck.

"*One* slice! And may I ask you for
Another drop of gravy?"
I sat and looked at him in awe,
For certainly I never saw
A thing so white and wavy.

And still he seemed to grow more white,
More vapoury, and wavier—
Seen in the dim and flickering light,
As he proceeded to recite
His 'Maxims of Behaviour'.

CANTO II: *Hys Fyve Rules*

"My First—but don't suppose," he said,
"I'm setting you a riddle—
Is—if your Victim be in bed,
Don't touch the curtains at his head,
But take them in the middle,

"And wave them slowly in and out,
While drawing them asunder;
And in a minute's time, no doubt,
He'll raise his head and look about
With eyes of wrath and wonder.

"And here you must on no pretence
Make the first observation.
Wait for the Victim to commence:
No Ghost of any common sense
Begins a conversation.

"If he should say 'How came you here?'
(The way that *you* began, Sir)
In such a case your course is clear—
'On the bat's back, my little dear!'
Is the appropriate answer.

"If after this he says no more,
You'd best perhaps curtail your
Exertions—go and shake the door,

And then, if he begins to snore,
You'll know the thing's a failure.

"By day, if he should be alone—
At home or on a walk—
You merely give a hollow groan,
To indicate the kind of tone
In which you mean to talk.

"But if you find him with his friends,
The thing is rather harder.
In such a case success depends
On picking up some candle-ends,
Or butter, in the larder.

"With this you make a kind of slide
(It answers best with suet),
On which you must contrive to glide,
And swing yourself from side to side—
One soon learns how to do it.

"The Second tells us what is right
In ceremonious calls:
First burn a blue or crimson light
(A thing I quite forgot to-night),
Then scratch the door or walls."

I said "You'll visit *here* no more,
If you attempt the Guy.

I'll have no bonfires on *my* floor—
And, as for scratching at the door,
I'd like to see you try!"

"The Third was written to protect
The interests of the Victim,
And tells us, as I recollect,
To treat him with a grave respect,
And not to contradict him."

"That's plain," said I, "as Tare and Tret,
To any comprehension:
I only wish *some* Ghosts I've met
Would not so *constantly* forget
The maxim that you mention!"

"Perhaps," he said, "*you* first transgressed
The laws of hospitality:
All Ghosts instinctively detest
The Man that fails to treat his guest
With proper cordiality.

"If you address a Ghost as 'Thing!'
Or strike him with a hatchet,
He is permitted by the King
To drop all formal parleying—
And then you're *sure* to catch it!

"The Fourth prohibits trespassing
Where other Ghosts are quartered:
And those convicted of the thing
(Unless when pardoned by the King)
Must instantly be slaughtered.

"That simply means 'be cut up small':
Ghosts soon unite anew.
The process scarcely hurts at all—
Not more than when *you*'re what you call
'Cut up' by a Review.

"The Fifth is one you may prefer
That I should quote entire:
The King must be addressed as 'Sir.'
This, from a simple courtier,
Is all the laws require:

"*But, should you wish to do the thing*
With out-and-out politeness,
Accost him as 'My Goblin King!
And always use, in answering,
The phrase 'Your Royal Whiteness!'

"I'm getting rather hoarse, I fear,
After so much reciting :
So, if you don't object, my dear,
We'll try a glass of bitter beer—
I think it looks inviting."

CANTO III: *Scarmoges*

"And did you really walk," said I,
"On such a wretched night?
I always fancied Ghosts could fly—
If not exactly in the sky,
Yet at a fairish height."

"It's very well," said he, "for Kings
To soar above the earth:
But Phantoms often find that wings—
Like many other pleasant things—
Cost more than they are worth.

"Spectres of course are rich, and so
Can buy them from the Elves:
But *we* prefer to keep below—
They're stupid company, you know,
For any but themselves:

"For, though they claim to be exempt
From pride, they treat a Phantom
As something quite beneath contempt—
Just as no Turkey ever dreamt
Of noticing a Bantam."

"They seem too proud," said I, "to go
To houses such as mine.
Pray, how did they contrive to know

So quickly that 'the place was low,'
And that I 'kept bad wine'?"

"Inspector Kobold came to you—"
The little Ghost began.
Here I broke in—"Inspector who?
Inspecting Ghosts is something new!
Explain yourself, my man!"

"His name is Kobold," said my guest:
"One of the Spectre order:
You'll very often see him dressed
In a yellow gown, a crimson vest,
And a night-cap with a border.

"He tried the Brocken business first,
But caught a sort of chill ;
So came to England to be nursed,
And here it took the form of *thirst*,
Which he complains of still.

"Port-wine, he says, when rich and sound,
Warms his old bones like nectar:
And as the inns, where it is found,
Are his especial hunting-ground,
We call him the *Inn-spectre*."

I bore it—bore it like a man—
This agonizing witticism!

And nothing could be sweeter than
My temper, till the Ghost began
Some most provoking criticism.

"Cooks need not be indulged in waste;
Yet still you'd better teach them
Dishes should have *some sort* of taste.
Pray, why are all the cruets placed
Where nobody can reach them?

"That man of yours will never earn
His living as a waiter!
Is that queer *thing* supposed to burn?
(It's far too dismal a concern
To call a Moderator).

"The duck was tender, but the peas
Were very much too old:
And just remember, if you please,
The *next* time you have toasted cheese,
Don't let them send it cold.

"You'd find the bread improved, I think,
By getting better flour:
And have you anything to drink
That looks a *little* less like ink,
And isn't *quite* so sour?"

Then, peering round with curious eyes,
He muttered "Goodness gracious!"
And so went on to criticise—
"Your room's an inconvenient size:
It's neither snug nor spacious.

"That narrow window, I expect,
Serves but to let the dusk in—"
"But please," said I, "to recollect
'Twas fashioned by an architect
Who pinned his faith on Ruskin!"

"I don't care who he was, Sir, or
On whom he pinned his faith!
Constructed by whatever law,
So poor a job I never saw,
As I'm a living Wraith!

"What a remarkable cigar!
How much are they a dozen?"
I growled "No matter what they are!
You're getting as familiar
As if you were my cousin!

"Now that's a thing I *will not stand*,
And so I tell you flat."
"Aha," said he, "we're getting grand!"
(Taking a bottle in his hand)
"I'll soon arrange for *that*!"

And here he took a careful aim,
And gaily cried "Here goes!"
I tried to dodge it as it came,
But somehow caught it, all the same,
Exactly on my nose.

And I remember nothing more
That I can clearly fix,
Till I was sitting on the floor,
Repeating "Two and five are four,
But *five and two* are six."

What really passed I never learned,
Nor guessed: I only know
That, when at last my sense returned,
The lamp, neglected, dimly burned—
The fire was getting low—

Through driving mists I seemed to see
A Thing that smirked and smiled:
And found that he was giving me
A lesson in Biography,
As if I were a child.

CANTO IV: *Hys Nouryture*

"Oh, when I was a little Ghost,
A merry time had we!

Each seated on his favourite post,
We chumped and chawed the buttered toast
They gave us for our tea."

"That story is in print!" I cried.
"Don't say it's not, because
It's known as well as Bradshaw's Guide!"
(The Ghost uneasily replied
He hardly thought it was).

"It's not in Nursery Rhymes? And yet
I almost think it is—
'Three little Ghosteses' were set
'On posteses,' you know, and ate
Their 'buttered toasteses.'

"I have the book; so if you doubt it—"
I turned to search the shelf.
"Don't stir!" he cried. "We'll do without it:
I now remember all about it;
I wrote the thing myself.

"It came out in a 'Monthly', or
At least my agent said it did:
Some literary swell, who saw
It, thought it seemed adapted for
The Magazine he edited.

"My father was a Brownie, Sir;
My mother was a Fairy.
The notion had occurred to her,
The children would be happier,
If they were taught to vary.

"The notion soon became a craze;
And, when it once began, she
Brought us all out in different ways—
One was a Pixy, two were Fays,
Another was a Banshee;

"The Fetch and Kelpie went to school
And gave a lot of trouble;
Next came a Poltergeist and Ghoul,
And then two Trolls (which broke the rule),
A Goblin, and a Double—

"(If that's a snuff-box on the shelf,"
He added with a yawn,
"I'll take a pinch)—next came an Elf,
And then a Phantom (that's myself),
And last, a Leprechaun.

"One day, some Spectres chanced to call,
Dressed in the usual white:
I stood and watched them in the hall,
And couldn't make them out at all,
They seemed so strange a sight.

"I wondered what on earth they were,
That looked all head and sack;
But Mother told me not to stare,
And then she twitched me by the hair,
And punched me in the back.

"Since then I've often wished that I
Had been a Spectre born.
But what's the use?" (He heaved a sigh.)
"*They* are the ghost-nobility,
And look on *us* with scorn.

"My phantom-life was soon begun:
When I was barely six,
I went out with an older one—
And just at first I thought it fun,
And learned a lot of tricks.

"I've haunted dungeons, castles, towers—
Wherever I was sent:
I've often sat and howled for hours,
Drenched to the skin with driving showers,
Upon a battlement.

"It's quite old-fashioned now to groan
When you begin to speak:
This is the newest thing in tone—"
And here (it chilled me to the bone)
He gave an *awful* squeak.

"Perhaps," he added, "to *your* ear
That sounds an easy thing?
Try it yourself, my little dear!
It took *me* something like a year,
With constant practising.

"And when you've learned to squeak, my man,
And caught the double sob,
You're pretty much where you began:
Just try and gibber if you can!
That's something *like* a job!

"*I've* tried it, and can only say
I'm sure you couldn't do it, e-
-ven if you practised night and day,
Unless you have a turn that way,
And natural ingenuity.

"Shakespeare I think it is who treats
Of Ghosts, in days of old,
Who 'gibbered in the Roman streets,'
Dressed, if you recollect, in sheets—
They must have found it cold.

"I've often spent ten pounds on stuff,
In dressing as a Double;
But, though it answers as a puff,
It never has effect enough
To make it worth the trouble.

"Long bills soon quenched the little thirst
I had for being funny.
The setting-up is always worst:
Such heaps of things you want at first,
One must be made of money!

"For instance, take a Haunted Tower,
With skull, cross-bones, and sheet;
Blue lights to burn (say) two an hour,
Condensing lens of extra power,
And set of chains complete:

"What with the things you have to hire,
The fitting on the robe
And testing all the coloured fire,
The outfit of itself would tire
The patience of a Job!

"And then they're so fastidious,
The Haunted-House Committee:
I've often known them make a fuss
Because a Ghost was French, or Russ,
Or even from the City!

"Some dialects are objected to—
For one, the Irish brogue is:
And then, for all you have to do,
One pound a week they offer you,
And find yourself in Bogies!

CANTO V: *Byckerment*

"Don't they consult the 'Victims,' though?"
I said. "They should, by rights,
Give them a chance—because, you know,
The tastes of people differ so,
Especially in Sprites."

The Phantom shook his head and smiled.
"Consult them? Not a bit!
'Twould be a job to drive one wild,
To satisfy one single child—
There'd be no end to it!"

"Of course you can't leave *children* free,"
Said I, "to pick and choose:
But, in the case of men like me,
I think 'Mine Host' might fairly be
Allowed to state his views."

He said "It really wouldn't pay—
Folk are so full of fancies.
We visit for a single day,
And whether then we go, or stay,
Depends on circumstances.

"And, though we don't consult 'Mine Host'
Before the thing's arranged,
Still, if he often quits his post,

Or is not a well-mannered Ghost,
Then you can have him changed.

"But if the host's a man like you—
I mean a man of sense;
And if the house is not too new—"
"Why, what has *that*," said I, "to do
With Ghost's convenience?"

"A new house does not suit, you know—
It's such a job to trim it:
But, after twenty years or so,
The wainscotings begin to go,
So twenty is the limit."

'To trim' was not a phrase I could
Remember having heard:
"Perhaps," I said, "you'll be so good
As tell me what is understood
Exactly by that word?"

"It means the loosening all the doors,"
The Ghost replied, and laughed:
"It means the drilling holes by scores
In all the skirting-boards and floors,
To make a thorough draught.

"You'll sometimes find that one or two
Are all you really need

To let the wind come whistling through—
But *here* there'll be a lot to do!"
I faintly gasped "Indeed!

"If I'd been rather later, I'll
Be bound," I added, trying
(Most unsuccessfully) to smile,
"You'd have been busy all this while,
Trimming and beautifying?"

"Why, no," said he; "perhaps I should
Have stayed another minute—
But still no Ghost, that's any good,
Without an introduction would
Have ventured to begin it.

"The proper thing, as you were late,
Was certainly to go:
But, with the roads in such a state,
I got the Knight-Mayor's leave to wait
For half an hour or so."

"Who's the Knight-Mayor?" I cried. Instead
Of answering my question,
"Well, if you don't know *that*," he said,
"Either you never go to bed,
Or you've a grand digestion!

"He goes about and sits on folk
That eat too much at night:
His duties are to pinch, and poke,
And squeeze them till they nearly choke."
(I said "It serves them right!")

"And folk who sup on things like these—"
He muttered, "eggs and bacon—
Lobster—and duck—and toasted cheese—
If they don't get an awful squeeze,
I'm very much mistaken!

"He is immensely fat, and so
Well suits the occupation:
In point of fact, if you must know,
We used to call him years ago,
The Mayor and Corporation!

"The day he was elected Mayor
I *know* that every Sprite meant
To vote for *me*, but did not dare—"
He was so frantic with despair
And furious with excitement.

"When it was over, for a whim,
He ran to tell the King;
And being the reverse of slim,
A two-mile trot was not for him
A very easy thing.

"So, to reward him for his run
(As it was baking hot,
And he was over twenty stone),
The King proceeded, half in fun,
To knight him on the spot."

" 'Twas a great liberty to take!"
(I fired up like a rocket).
"He did it just for punning's sake:
'The man,' says Johnson, 'that would make
A pun, would pick a pocket!' "

"A man," said he, "is not a King."
I argued for a while,
And did my best to prove the thing—
The Phantom merely listening
With a contemptuous smile.

At last, when, breath and patience spent,
I had recourse to smoking—
"Your *aim*," he said, "is excellent:
But—when you call it *argument* —
Of course you're only joking?"

Stung by his cold and snaky eye,
I roused myself at length
To say "At least I do defy
The veriest sceptic to deny
That union is strength!"

"That's true enough," said he, "yet stay—"
I listened in all meekness—
"*Union* is strength, I'm bound to say;
In fact, the thing's as clear as day;
But *Onions* are a weakness."

CANTO VI: *Dyscomfyture*

As one who strives a hill to climb,
Who never climbed before:
Who finds it, in a little time,
Grow every moment less sublime,
And votes the thing a bore:

Yet, having once begun to try,
Dares not desert his quest,
But, climbing, ever keeps his eye
On one small hut against the sky
Wherein he hopes to rest:

Who climbs till nerve and force are spent,
With many a puff and pant:
Who still, as rises the ascent,
In language grows more violent,
Although in breath more scant:

Who, climbing, gains at length the place
That crowns the upward track.

And, entering with unsteady pace,
Receives a buffet in the face
That lands him on his back:

And feels himself, like one in sleep,
Glide swiftly down again,
A helpless weight, from steep to steep,
Till, with a headlong giddy sweep,
He drops upon the plain—

So I, that had resolved to bring
Conviction to a ghost,
And found it quite a different thing
From any human arguing,
Yet dared not quit my post

But, keeping still the end in view
To which I hoped to come,
I strove to prove the matter true
By putting everything I knew
Into an axiom:

Commencing every single phrase
With 'therefore' or 'because,'
I blindly reeled, a hundred ways,
About the syllogistic maze,
Unconscious where I was.

Quoth he "That's regular clap-trap:
Don't bluster any more.
Now *do* be cool and take a nap!
Such a ridiculous old chap
Was never seen before!

"You're like a man I used to meet,
Who got one day so furious
In arguing, the simple heat
Scorched both his slippers off his feet!"
I said "*That's very curious!*"

"Well, it *is* curious, I agree,
And sounds perhaps like fibs:
But still it's true as true can be—
As sure as your name's Tibbs," said he.
I said "My name's *not* Tibbs."

"*Not* Tibbs!" he cried—his tone became
A shade or two less hearty—
"Why, no," said I. "My proper name
Is Tibbets—" "Tibbets?" "Aye, the same."
"Why, then *you're not the party!*"

With that he struck the board a blow
That shivered half the glasses.
"Why couldn't you have told me so
Three quarters of an hour ago,
You prince of all the asses?

"To walk four miles through mud and rain,
To spend the night in smoking,
And then to find that it's in vain—
And I've to do it all again—
It's really *too* provoking!

"Don't talk!" he cried, as I began
To mutter some excuse.
"Who can have patience with a man
That's got no more discretion than
An idiotic goose?

"To keep me waiting here, instead
Of telling me at once
That this was not the house!" he said.
"There, that'll do—be off to bed!
Don't gape like that, you dunce!"

"It's very fine to throw the blame
On *me* in such a fashion!
Why didn't you enquire my name
The very minute that you came?"
I answered in a passion.

"Of course it worries you a bit
To come so far on foot—
But how was I to blame for it?"
"Well, well!" said he. "I must admit
That isn't badly put.

"And certainly you've given me
The best of wine and victual—
Excuse my violence," said he,
"But accidents like this, you see,
They put one out a little.

"'Twas *my* fault after all, I find—
Shake hands, old Turnip-top!"
The name was hardly to my mind,
But, as no doubt he meant it kind,
I let the matter drop.

"Good-night, old Turnip-top, good-night!
When I am gone, perhaps
They'll send you some inferior Sprite,
Who'll keep you in a constant fright
And spoil your soundest naps.

"Tell him you'll stand no sort of trick;
Then, if he leers and chuckles,
You just be handy with a stick
(Mind that it's pretty hard and thick)
And rap him on the knuckles!

"Then carelessly remark 'Old coon!
Perhaps you're not aware
That, if you don't behave, you'll soon
Be chuckling to another tune—
And so you'd best take care!'

"That's the right way to cure a Sprite
Of such like goings-on—
But gracious me! It's getting light!
Good-night, old Turnip-top, good-night!"
A nod, and he was gone.

CANTO VII: *Sad Souvenaunce*

"What's this?" I pondered. "Have I slept?
Or can I have been drinking?"
But soon a gentler feeling crept
Upon me, and I sat and wept
An hour or so, like winking.

"No need for Bones to hurry so!"
I sobbed. "In fact, I doubt
If it was worth his while to go—
And who is Tibbs, I'd like to know,
To make such work about?

"If Tibbs is anything like me,
It's *possible*," I said,
"He won't be over-pleased to be
Dropped in upon at half-past three,
After he's snug in bed.

"And if Bones plagues him anyhow—
Squeaking and all the rest of it,

As he was doing here just now—
I prophesy there'll be a row,
And Tibbs will have the best of it!"

Then, as my tears could never bring
The friendly Phantom back,
It seemed to me the proper thing
To mix another glass, and sing
The following Coronach.

"And art thou gone, beloved ghost?
Best of familiars!
Nay then, farewell, my duckling roast,
Farewell, farewell, my tea and toast,
My meerschaum and cigars!

"The hues of life are dull and grey,
The sweets of life insipid,
When thou, *my charmer, art away—*
Old brick, or rather, let me say,
Old parallelepiped!"

Instead of singing Verse the Third,
I ceased—abruptly, rather:
But, after such a splendid word
I felt that it would be absurd
To try it any farther.

So with a yawn I went my way
To seek the welcome downy,
And slept, and dreamed till break of day
Of Poltergeist and Fetch and Fay
And Leprechaun and Brownie!

For year I've not been visited
By any kind of Sprite;
Yet still they echo in my head,
Those parting words, so kindly said,
"Old Turnip-top, good-night!"

THE HUNTING OF THE SNARK

"Just the place for a Snark!" the Bellman cried,
As he landed his crew with care;
Supporting each man on the top of the tide
By a finger entwined in his hair.

"Just the place for a Snark! I have said it twice:
That alone should encourage the crew.
Just the place for a Snark! I have said it thrice:
What I tell you three times is true."

The crew was complete: it included a Boots—
A maker of Bonnets and Hoods—
A Barrister, brought to arrange their disputes,
And a Broker, to value their goods.

A Billiard-marker, whose skill was immense,
Might perhaps have won more than his share,
But a Banker, engaged at enormous expense,
Had the whole of their cash in his care.

There was also a Beaver, that paced on the deck,
Or would sit making lace in the bow:
And had often (the Bellman said) saved them from
    wreck,
Though none of the sailors knew how.

There was one who was famed for the number of
    things
He forgot when he entered the ship:
His umbrella, his watch, all his jewels and rings,
And the clothes he had bought for the trip.

He had forty-two boxes, all carefully packed,
With his name painted clearly on each:
But, since he omitted to mention the fact,
They were all left behind on the beach.

The loss of his clothes hardly mattered, because
He had seven coats on when he came,
With three pair of boots—but the worst of it was,
He had wholly forgotten his name.

He would answer to 'Hi!' or to any loud cry,
Such as 'Fry me!' or 'Fritter my wig!'
To 'What-you-may-call-um!' or 'What-was-his-
    name!'
But especially 'Thing-um-a-jig!'

While, for those who preferred a more forcible word,
He had different names from these:
His intimate friends called him 'Candle-ends,'
And his enemies 'Toasted-cheese.'

"His form in ungainly—his intellect small—"
(So the Bellman would often remark)

"But his courage is perfect! And that, after all,
Is the thing that one needs with a Snark."

He would joke with hyenas, returning their stare
With an impudent wag of the head:
And he once went a walk, paw-in-paw, with a bear,
"Just to keep up its spirits," he said.

He came as a Baker: but owned, when too late—
And it drove the poor Bellman half-mad—
He could only bake Bridecake—for which, I may
    state,
No materials were to be had.

The last of the crew needs especial remark,
Though he looked an incredible dunce:
He had just one idea—but, that one being 'Snark',
The good Bellman engaged him at once.

He came as a Butcher: but gravely declared,
When the ship had been sailing a week,
He could only kill Beavers. The Bellman looked
    scared,
And was almost too frightened to speak:

But at length he explained, in a tremulous tone,
There was only one Beaver on board;
And that was a tame one he had of his own,
Whose death would be deeply deplored.

The Beaver, who happened to hear the remark,
Protested, with tears in its eyes,
That not even the rapture of hunting the Snark
Could atone for that dismal surprise!

It strongly advised that the Butcher should be
Conveyed in a separate ship:
But the Bellman declared that would never agree
With the plans he had made for the trip:

Navigation was always a difficult art,
Though with only one ship and one bell:
And he feared he must really decline, for his part,
Undertaking another as well.

The Beaver's best course was, no doubt, to procure
A second-hand dagger-proof coat—
So the Baker advised it—and next, to insure
Its life in some Office of note:

This the Banker suggested, and offered for hire
(On moderate terms) or for sale,
Two excellent Policies, one Against Fire,
And one Against Damage From Hail.

Yet still, ever after that sorrowful day,
Whenever the Butcher was by,
The Beaver kept looking the opposite way,
And appeared unaccountably shy.

FIT THE SECOND: *The Bellman's Speech*

The Bellman himself they all praised to the skies—
Such a carriage, such ease and such grace!
Such solemnity, too! One could see he was wise,
The moment one looked in his face!

He had bought a large map representing the sea,
Without the least vestige of land:
And the crew were much pleased when they found it
    to be
A map they could all understand.

"What's the good of Mercator's North Poles and
    Equators,
Tropics, Zones, and Meridian Lines?"
So the Bellman would cry: and the crew would reply
"They are merely conventional signs!

"Other maps are such shapes, with their islands and
    capes!
But we've got our brave Captain to thank"
(So the crew would protest) "that he's bought us the
    best—
A perfect and absolute blank!"

This was charming, no doubt; but they shortly found
    out
That the Captain they trusted so well

Had only one notion for crossing the ocean,
And that was to tingle his bell.

He was thoughtful and grave—but the orders he gave
Were enough to bewilder a crew.
When he cried "Steer to starboard, but keep her
    head larboard!"
What on earth was the helmsman to do?

Then the bowsprit got mixed with the rudder
    sometimes:
A thing, as the Bellman remarked,
That frequently happens in tropical climes,
When a vessel is, so to speak, 'snarked'.

But the principal failing occurred in the sailing,
And the Bellman, perplexed and distressed,
Said he had hoped, at least, when the wind blew due
    East,
That the ship would not travel due West!

But the danger was past—they had landed at last,
With their boxes, portmanteaus, and bags:
Yet at first sight the crew were not pleased with the
    view,
Which consisted of chasms and crags.

The Bellman perceived that their spirits were low,
And repeated in musical tone

Some jokes he had kept for a season of woe—
But the crew would do nothing but groan.

He served out some grog with a liberal hand,
And bade them sit down on the beach:
And they could not but own that their Captain
looked grand,
As he stood and delivered his speech.

"Friends, Romans, and countrymen, lend me your
ears!"
(They were all of them fond of quotations:
So they drank to his health, and they gave him three
cheers,
While he served out additional rations).

"We have sailed many months, we have sailed many
weeks,
(Four weeks to the month you may mark),
But never as yet ('tis your Captain who speaks)
Have we caught the least glimpse of a Snark!

"We have sailed many weeks, we have sailed many
days,
(Seven days to the week I allow),
But a Snark, on the which we might lovingly gaze,
We have never beheld till now!

"Come, listen, my men, while I tell you again
The five unmistakable marks
By which you may know, wheresoever you go,
The warranted genuine Snarks.

"Let us take them in order. The first is the taste,
Which is meagre and hollow, but crisp:
Like a coat that is rather too tight in the waist,
With a flavour of Will-o-the-wisp.

"Its habit of getting up late you'll agree
That it carries too far, when I say
That it frequently breakfasts at five-o'clock tea,
And dines on the following day.

"The third is its slowness in taking a jest.
Should you happen to venture on one,
It will sigh like a thing that is deeply distressed:
And it always looks grave at a pun.

"The fourth is its fondness for bathing-machines,
Which it constantly carries about,
And believes that they add to the beauty of scenes—
A sentiment open to doubt.

"The fifth is ambition. It next will be right
To describe each particular batch:
Distinguishing those that have feathers, and bite,
From those that have whiskers, and scratch.

"For, although common Snarks do no manner of
  harm,
Yet, I feel it my duty to say,
Some are Boojums—" The Bellman broke off in
  alarm,
For the Baker had fainted away.

FIT THE THIRD: *The Baker's Tale*

They roused him with muffins—they roused him
  with ice;
They roused him with mustard and cress;
They roused him with jam and judicious advice;
They set him conundrums to guess.

When at length he sat up and was able to speak,
His sad story he offered to tell;
And the Bellman cried "Silence! Not even a shriek!"
And excitedly tingled his bell.

There was silence supreme! Not a shriek, not a
  scream,
Scarcely even a howl or a groan,
As the man they called 'Ho!' told his story of woe
In an antediluvian tone.

"My father and mother were honest, though poor—"
"Skip all that!" cried the Bellman in haste.

"If it once becomes dark, there's no chance of a
    Snark—
We have hardly a minute to waste!"

"I skip forty years," said the Baker, in tears,
"And proceed without further remark
To the day when you took me aboard of your ship
To help you in hunting the Snark.

"A dear uncle of mine (after whom I was named)
Remarked, when I bade him farewell—"
"Oh, skip your dear uncle!" the Bellman exclaimed,
As he angrily tingled his bell.

"He remarked to me then," said that mildest of men,
" 'If your Snark be a Snark, that is right:
Fetch it home by all means—you may serve it with
    greens,
And it's handy for striking a light.

" 'You may seek it with thimbles—and seek it with
    care;
You may hunt it with forks and hope;
You may threaten its life with a railway-share;
You may charm it with smiles and soap—' "

("That's exactly the method," the Bellman bold
In a hasty parenthesis cried,
"That's exactly the way I have always been told
That the capture of Snarks should be tried!")

" 'But oh, beamish nephew, beware of the day,
If your Snark be a Boojum! For then
You will softly and suddenly vanish away,
And never be met with again!'

"It is this, it is this that oppresses my soul,
When I think of my uncle's last words:
And my heart is like nothing so much as a bowl
Brimming over with quivering curds!

"It is this, it is this—" "We have had that before!"
The Bellman indignantly said.
And the Baker replied "Let me say it once more.
It is this, it is this that I dread!

"I engage with the Snark—every night after dark—
In a dreamy delirious fight:
I serve it with greens in those shadowy scenes,
And I use it for striking a light:

"But if ever I meet with a Boojum, that day,
In a moment (of this I am sure),
I shall softly and suddenly vanish away—
And the notion I cannot endure!"

FIT THE FOURTH: *The Hunting*

The Bellman looked uffish, and wrinkled his brow.
"If only you'd spoken before!

It's excessively awkward to mention it now,
With the Snark, so to speak, at the door!

"We should all of us grieve, as you well may believe,
If you never were met with again—
But surely, my man, when the voyage began,
You might have suggested it then?

"It's excessively awkward to mention it now—
As I think I've already remarked."
And the man they called 'Hi!' replied, with a sigh,
"I informed you the day we embarked.

"You may charge me with murder—or want of
      sense—
(We are all of us weak at times):
But the slightest approach to a false pretence
Was never among my crimes!

"I said it in Hebrew—I said it in Dutch—
I said it in German and Greek:
But I wholly forgot (and it vexes me much)
That English is what you speak!"

" 'Tis a pitiful tale," said the Bellman, whose face
Had grown longer at every word:
"But, now that you've stated the whole of your case,
More debate would be simply absurd.

"The rest of my speech" (he explained to his men)
"You shall hear when I've leisure to speak it.
But the Snark is at hand, let me tell you again!
'Tis your glorious duty to seek it!

"To seek it with thimbles, to seek it with care;
To pursue it with forks and hope;
To threaten its life with a railway-share;
To charm it with smiles and soap!

"For the Snark's a peculiar creature, that won't
Be caught in a commonplace way.
Do all that you know, and try all that you don't:
Not a chance must be wasted today!

"For England expects—I forbear to proceed:
'Tis a maxim tremendous, but trite:
And you'd best be unpacking the things that you need
To rig yourselves out for the fight."

Then the Banker endorsed a blank cheque (which he
    crossed),
And changed his loose silver for notes.
The Baker with care combed his whiskers and hair,
And shook the dust out of his coats.

The Boots and the Broker were sharpening a
    spade—
Each working the grindstone in turn:

But the Beaver went on making lace, and displayed
No interest in the concern:

Though the Barrister tried to appeal to its pride,
And vainly proceeded to cite
A number of cases, in which making laces
Had been proved an infringement of right.

The maker of Bonnets ferociously planned
A novel arrangement of bows:
While the Billiard-marker with quivering hand
Was chalking the tip of his nose.

But the Butcher turned nervous, and dressed himself
    fine,
With yellow kid gloves and a ruff—
Said he felt it exactly like going to dine,
Which the Bellman declared was all 'stuff'.

"Introduce me, now there's a good fellow," he said,
"If we happen to meet it together!"
And the Bellman, sagaciously nodding his head,
Said "That must depend on the weather."

The Beaver went simply galumphing about,
At seeing the Butcher so shy:
And even the Baker, though stupid and stout,
Made an effort to wink with one eye.

"Be a man!" said the Bellman in wrath, as he heard
The Butcher beginning to sob.
"Should we meet with a Jubjub, that desperate bird,
We shall need all our strength for the job!"

FIT THE FIFTH: *The Beaver's Lesson*

They sought it with thimbles, they sought it with
    care;
They pursued it with forks and hope;
They threatened its life with a railway-share;
They charmed it with smiles and soap.

Then the Butcher contrived an ingenious plan
For making a separate sally;
And had fixed on a spot unfrequented by man,
A dismal and desolate valley.

But the very same plan to the Beaver occurred:
It had chosen the very same place:
Yet neither betrayed, by a sign or a word,
The disgust that appeared in his face.

Each thought he was thinking of nothing but 'Snark'
And the glorious work of the day;
And each tried to pretend that he did not remark
That the other was going that way.

But the valley grew narrow and narrower still,
And the evening got darker and colder,
Till (merely from nervousness, not from goodwill)
They marched along shoulder to shoulder.

Then a scream, shrill and high, rent the shuddering
    sky,
And they knew that some danger was near:
The Beaver turned pale to the tip of its tail,
And even the Butcher felt queer.

He thought of his childhood, left far far behind—
That blissful and innocent state—
The sound so exactly recalled to his mind
A pencil that squeaks on a slate!

" 'Tis the voice of the Jubjub!" he suddenly cried.
(This man, that they used to call 'Dunce.')
"As the Bellman would tell you," he added with
    pride,
"I have uttered that sentiment once.

" 'Tis the note of the Jubjub! Keep count, I entreat;
You will find I have told it you twice.
'Tis the song of the Jubjub! The proof is complete,
If only I've stated it thrice."

The Beaver had counted with scrupulous care,
Attending to every word:

But it fairly lost heart, and outgrabe in despair,
When the third repetition occurred.

It felt that, in spite of all possible pains,
It had somehow contrived to lose count,
And the only thing now was to rack its poor brains
By reckoning up the amount.

"Two added to one—if that could but be done,"
It said, "with one's fingers and thumbs!"
Recollecting with tears how, in earlier years,
It had taken no pains with its sums.

"The thing can be done," said the Butcher, "I think.
The thing must be done, I am sure.
The thing shall be done! Bring me paper and ink,
The best there is time to procure."

The Beaver brought paper, portfolio, pens,
And ink in unfailing supplies:
While strange creepy creatures came out of their
    dens,
And watched them with wondering eyes.

So engrossed was the Butcher, he heeded them not,
As he wrote with a pen in each hand,
And explained all the while in a popular style
Which the Beaver could well understand.

"Taking Three as the subject to reason about—
A convenient number to state—
We add Seven, and Ten, and then multiply out
By One Thousand diminished by Eight.

"The result we proceed to divide, as you see,
By Nine Hundred and Ninety and Two:
Then subtract Seventeen, and the answer must be
Exactly and perfectly true.

"The method employed I would gladly explain,
While I have it so clear in my head,
If I had but the time and you had but the brain—
But much yet remains to be said.

"In one moment I've seen what has hitherto been
Enveloped in absolute mystery,
And without extra charge I will give you at large
A Lesson in Natural History."

In his genial way he proceeded to say
(Forgetting all laws of propriety,
And that giving instruction, without introduction,
Would have caused quite a thrill in Society),

"As to temper the Jubjub's a desperate bird,
Since it lives in perpetual passion;
Its taste in costume is entirely absurd—
It is ages ahead of the fashion;

"But it knows any friend it has met once before:
It never will look at a bride;
And in charity-meetings it stands at the door,
And collects—though it does not subscribe.

"Its flavour when cooked is more exquisite far
Than mutton, or oysters, or eggs
(Some think it keeps best in an ivory jar,
And some, in mahogany kegs);

"You boil it in sawdust; you salt it in glue;
You condense it with locusts and tape;
Still keeping one principal object in view—
To preserve its symmetrical shape."

The Butcher would gladly have talked till next day,
But he felt that the Lesson must end,
And he wept with delight in attempting to say
He considered the Beaver his friend.

While the Beaver confessed, with affectionate looks
More eloquent even than tears,
It had learned in ten minutes far more than all books
Would have taught it in seventy years.

They returned hand-in-hand, and the Bellman,
     unmanned
(For a moment) with noble emotion,
Said "This amply repays all the wearisome days
We have spent on the billowy ocean!"

Such friends, as the Beaver and Butcher became,
Have seldom if ever been known;
In winter or summer, 'twas always the same—
You could never meet either alone.

And when quarrels arose—as one frequently finds
Quarrels will, spite of every endeavour—
The song of the Jubjub recurred to their minds,
And cemented their friendship for ever!

FIT THE SIXTH: *The Barrister's Dream*

They sought it with thimbles, they sought it with
     care;
They pursued it with forks and hope;
They threatened its life with a railway-share;
They charmed it with smiles and soap.

But the Barrister, weary of proving in vain
That the Beaver's lace-making was wrong,
Fell asleep, and in dreams saw the creature quite plain
That his fancy had dwelt on so long.

He dreamed that he stood in a shadowy Court,
Where the Snark, with a glass in its eye,
Dressed in gown, bands, and wig, was defending a pig
On the charge of deserting its sty.

The Witnesses proved, without error or flaw,
That the sty was deserted when found:
And the Judge kept explaining the state of the law
In a soft under-current of sound.

The indictment had never been clearly expressed,
And it seemed that the Snark had begun,
And had spoken three hours, before any one guessed
What the pig was supposed to have done.

The Jury had each formed a different view
(Long before the indictment was read),
And they all spoke at once, so that none of them knew
One word that the others had said.

"You must know —" said the Judge: but the Snark
    exclaimed "Fudge!
That statute is obsolete quite!
Let me tell you, my friends, the whole question
    depends
On an ancient manorial right.

"In the matter of Treason the pig would appear
To have aided, but scarcely abetted:
While the charge of Insolvency fails, it is clear,
If you grant the plea "never indebted".

"The fact of Desertion I will not dispute;
But its guilt, as I trust, is removed

(So far as relates to the costs of this suit)
By the Alibi which has been proved.

"My poor client's fate now depends on your votes."
Here the speaker sat down in his place,
And directed the Judge to refer to his notes
And briefly to sum up the case.

But the Judge said he never had summed up before;
So the Snark undertook it instead,
And summed it so well that it came to far more
Than the Witnesses ever had said!

When the verdict was called for, the Jury declined,
As the word was so puzzling to spell;
But they ventured to hope that the Snark wouldn't
    mind
Undertaking that duty as well.

So the Snark found the verdict, although, as it owned,
It was spent with the toils of the day:
When it said the word "*Guilty!*" the Jury all groaned,
And some of them fainted away.

Then the Snark pronounced sentence, the Judge
    being quite
Too nervous to utter a word:
When it rose to its feet, there was silence like night,
And the fall of a pin might be heard.

"Transportation for life" was the sentence it gave,
"And then to be fined forty pound."
The Jury all cheered, though the Judge said he feared
That the phrase was not legally sound.

But their wild exultation was suddenly checked
When the jailer informed them, with tears,
Such a sentence would have not the slightest effect,
As the pig had been dead for some years.

The Judge left the Court, looking deeply disgusted:
But the Snark, though a little aghast,
As the lawyer to whom the defence was intrusted,
Went bellowing on to the last.

Thus the Barrister dreamed, while the bellowing seemed
To grow every moment more clear:
Till he woke to the knell of a furious bell,
Which the Bellman rang close at his ear.

FIT THE SEVENTH: *The Banker's Fate*

They sought it with thimbles, they sought it with care;
They pursued it with forks and hope;
They threatened its life with a railway-share;
They charmed it with smiles and soap.

And the Banker, inspired with a courage so new
It was matter for general remark,
Rushed madly ahead and was lost to their view
In his zeal to discover the Snark

But while he was seeking with thimbles and care,
A Bandersnatch swiftly drew nigh
And grabbed at the Banker, who shrieked in despair,
For he knew it was useless to fly.

He offered large discount—he offered a cheque
(Drawn 'to bearer') for seven-pounds-ten:
But the Bandersnatch merely extended its neck
And grabbed at the Banker again.

Without rest or pause—while those frumious jaws
Went savagely snapping around—
He skipped and he hopped, and he floundered and
    flopped,
Till fainting he fell to the ground.

The Bandersnatch fled as the others appeared
Led on by that fear-stricken yell;
And the Bellman remarked "It is just as I feared!"
And solemnly tolled on his bell.

He was black in the face, and they scarcely could
    trace
The least likeness to what he had been:

While so great was his fright that his waistcoat turned
    white—
A wonderful thing to be seen!

To the horror of all who were present that day,
He uprose in full evening dress,
And with senseless grimaces endeavoured to say
What his tongue could no longer express.

Down he sank in a chair—ran his hands through his
    hair—
And chanted in mimsiest tones
Words whose utter inanity proved his insanity,
While he rattled a couple of bones.

"Leave him here to his fate—it is getting so late!"
The Bellman exclaimed in a fright.
"We have lost half the day. Any further delay,
And we shan't catch a Snark before night!"

FIT THE EIGHTH: *The Vanishing*

They sought it with thimbles, they sought it with
    care;
They pursued it with forks and hope;
They threatened its life with a railway-share;
They charmed it with smiles and soap.

They shuddered to think that the chase might fail,
And the Beaver, excited at last,
Went bounding along on the tip of its tail,
For the daylight was nearly past.

"There is Thingumbob shouting!" the Bellman said,
"He is shouting like mad, only hark!
He is waving his hands, he is wagging his head,
He has certainly found a Snark!"

They gazed in delight, while the Butcher exclaimed
"He was always a desperate wag!"
They beheld him—their Baker—their hero
    unnamed—
On the top of a neighbouring crag,

Erect and sublime, for one moment of time
In the next, that wild figure they saw
(As if stung by a spasm) plunge into a chasm,
While they waited and listened in awe.

"It's a Snark!" was the sound that first came to their
    ears,
And seemed almost too good to be true.
Then followed a torrent of laughter and cheers:
Then the ominous words "It's a Boo—"

Then, silence. Some fancied they heard in the air
A weary and wandering sigh

Then sounded like "—jum!" but the others declare
It was only a breeze that went by.

They hunted till darkness came on, but they found
Not a button, or feather, or mark,
By which they could tell that they stood on the
    ground
Where the Baker had met with the Snark.

In the midst of the word he was trying to say,
In the midst of his laughter and glee,
He had softly and suddenly vanished away—
For the Snark was a Boojum, you see.

THE END

Lightning Source UK Ltd.
Milton Keynes UK
UKOW04f0840180913

217436UK00001B/19/A